Praise for *Disrupt Politics*

"**Disrupt Politics** identifies clearly a rising and necessary movement in America to change our politics and disrupt the status quo party system. James Strock reveals the hunger among citizens for a new way of governance—and one that that harkens back to our Constitution."

—Matthew Dowd, Chief Political Analyst, ABC News

"America is in transition—and the old rules are out the window. 21st century leaders in government and politics must adapt to the new paradigm or fade away. **Disrupt Politics** is a reliable roadmap for continued American preeminence."

—Matt K. Lewis, senior columnist, *The Daily Beast*

"James Strock draws from a lifetime of political and government experience to sketch a portrait of a broken system that is thoughtful, provocative and insightful. At a time when too many Americans are simply despairing at what politics has become, **Disrupt Politics** offers a path forward."

—Dan Schnur, Director, Jesse M. Unruh Institute of Politics, USC

"**Disrupt Politics** is full of compelling ideas, including the big one: the only way to fix broken government is to rebuild it."

—Philip K. Howard, author, *The Death of Comm*

Disrupt Politics

The Spirit of '76, by Archibald Willard, ca. 1875

Disrupt Politics

Reset Washington

James Strock

Serve to Lead Group

By James Strock

Disrupt Politics

Serve to Lead

Theodore Roosevelt on Leadership

Reagan on Leadership

Published in the United States of America by the Serve to Lead Group
http://servetolead.org
Previously released as *disruptpolitics.us*

ISBN-10: 0984077472
ISBN-13: 9780984077472 (pbk.)

Printed in the United States of America

Author Photo: April Bennett | Soul's Image
Cover Design: Amanda Regan

For Rachel and Charles Bernheim

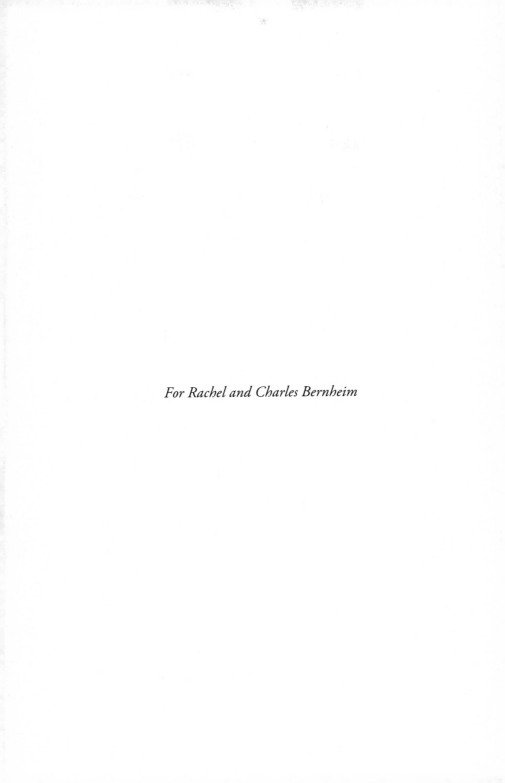

Remember this lesson. History does not teach fatalism. There are moments when the will of a handful of free men breaks through determinism and opens up new roads. People get the history they deserve.

— Charles de Gaulle

Contents

Foreword: 2017 Edition

We are not merely transferring power from one administration to another or from one party to another, but we are transferring power from Washington, D.C. and giving it back to you, the people.

For too long, a small group in our nation's capital has reaped the rewards of government while the people have borne the cost. Washington flourished, but the people did not share in its wealth. Politicians prospered, but the jobs left and the factories closed. The establishment protected itself, but not the citizens of the country. Their victories have not been your victories. Their triumphs have not been your triumphs. And while they celebrated in the nation's capital, there was little to celebrate for struggling families all across our land.

—President Donald Trump, January 20, 2017

The disruption of our politics has begun.

On November 8, 2016, an electoral earthquake rattled the very structure of American governance.

As the dust cleared, the Bush, Clinton and Obama political machines lay in smoldering wreckage. They will not rise again in the same forms.

The privileged beneficiaries of the passing order lament the end of an era. Their invincible sense of entitlement blinded them to the rising sense of disenfranchisement among millions of Americans over the preceding quarter century.

The new order in Washington will be led by a figure who defies longstanding norms. Donald Trump stands as the first president who has held no public office. He did not serve in the military. He is at best loosely affiliated with the Republican Party. He seized it in a hostile takeover. Many in the GOP "establishment" preferred electoral defeat to the prospect of his presidency. In all essentials, Trump is an independent. He is in the Republican Party, but not of it.

Nor was a he a one-off. Senator Bernie Sanders, an independent who caucuses with Democrats, came achingly close to winning the Democratic presidential nomination. In the face of a process that was, by any objective reckoning, "rigged," Sanders persevered. He was a most unlikely insurgent. No hard-headed political consultant would have turned to a rumpled, plain-speaking, septuagenarian and self-described socialist from Vermont to challenge the uniformly arrayed power centers of the Democratic Party. Nonetheless, Sanders defeated the anointed Hillary Clinton in twenty-three nominating contests.

The rejection of entrenched elites is not limited to the United States. In June 2016, the English people defied expectations, voting for "Brexit," a referendum to separate from the European Union. Longstanding political alignments in other nations are also buckling under evident stress.

Defender or Threat to the Constitution?

In the aftermath of his election, numerous mainstream commentators have asserted that Trump poses a challenge to our system of government. His heedless, at times gleeful trampling of longstanding norms is seen as a threat to liberal democracy itself.

His supporters respond that Trump is not opposing our constitutional system at all. In their view, he seeks to restore it, following the damage done by the political class.

Disrupt Politics argues that our constitutional machinery has been seized by the Special Interest State. It diagnoses dysfunctions that can be cured by reviving neglected constitutional arrangements and understandings. Fortunately, the underlying assumptions of the Constitution—decentralized and divided powers, reliance on extensive citizen participation in self-government—are well-suited for our twenty-first-century, digital age.

The challenges outlined in the book constitute a tremendous leadership opportunity for the president.

A Speech for a President

Though I could not have known when I wrote this book, more and more people shared the sentiment—varying from concern to outrage—that the political system was primed to offer up yet another Bush-Clinton presidential election in 2016.

Many readers said that *Disrupt Politics* opened their eyes to the full reach of the Special Interest State. Some, though, drew a conclusion that I did not foresee or intend. They fear that the elites are so deeply entrenched that reform is futile.

Are we prepared to succumb to such defeatism? Earlier generations fought the odds to restore our constitutional values amid new circumstances. So can we.

The 2016 election results will be interpreted by many people in many ways. What's indisputable is that the American people are demanding change. Many of us are manifestly willing to take rather large risks for it.

Donald Trump succeeded in disrupting the presidential selection process. Now the question is, can he disrupt our politics in a manner that will transform our government?

The president is the sole elected official who represents all Americans. As such, it falls to him or her to lead the disruption. Adding to the challenge, the chief executive must simultaneously ensure that that the ongoing tasks of government are being performed effectively.

This is no small feat. But it can be done. It requires presidential leadership, representing the demands, desires and values of We the People.

Paradoxically, transformational change may be more achievable than piecemeal efforts. Small changes can readily be absorbed by the broader system of the Special Interest State. In addition, absent a shared, inspiring vision, citizen participation and support would be difficult to elicit or sustain.

What would such leadership look like? Here's one take, in the form of a draft presidential address:

Disrupt Politics: Reset Washington
An Address by the President
The White House
Washington

My fellow citizens, I would like to speak with you about a fundamental commitment of my administration: draining the swamp in Washington, DC.

Having served in the White House for some months, I've seen first-hand that changing the system will be even harder than anyone might imagine.

That means we're going to have to work harder, work smarter, and be more tenacious than we ever have before.

Draining the swamp is something that no one can accomplish alone. Not even a president. Your participation—your leadership—is needed.

The stakes are high. Until we update and upgrade the foundation of our politics, whatever policies we build will be precarious. The great challenges that the politicians have failed to address for more than a generation—from the massive debt, to the breakdown of our immigration system, to secret trade deals drafted in darkness—are outcomes of our broken system.

I pledge that I will work with you and for you, hour by hour, day by day, to drain the swamp, to change the system.

The stakes could not be higher.

The Fundamental Question

The founders of our nation asked: Will we accept being subjects? Or will We the People rule ourselves as citizens?

Serving you from the White House, I constantly ask: Will government serve the people? Or will the people continue to endure the rule by the elites who have taken control of Washington in recent decades?

This question is as old as our nation and as current as a Twitter feed. Several generations have been faced with updating the American experiment in self-rule amid new circumstances. This was the great challenge before our first president, George Washington. It was later confronted by his most consequential successors, including Andrew

Jackson, Abraham Lincoln, Theodore Roosevelt, Woodrow Wilson, Franklin Roosevelt, and Ronald Reagan.

Now, we face this challenge at the dawn of the 21st century. How we respond will have consequences for those who come after us.

Four Commitments

To do my part, I make four commitments to you:

1. Your government will serve you—not the other way around.
2. Politicians and other office holders will live and work under the laws they set for the rest of us.
3. Our public institutions will be updated to meet the needs of our time.
4. Government will be transparent, enabling you, the citizens we serve, to participate and guide it.

Let us go through each of these in turn.

Government Will Serve the People

A courageous group of citizens declared independence from Great Britain in 1776. They balked at distant government from London. They were outraged by swarms of office holders who interfered with their lives and livelihoods.

From the point of view of the elites who ran the colonial system, the American revolutionaries were the original "deplorables."

Against all odds, the Americans defeated the most powerful military machine on earth.

The first words of our Constitution are: *We the People*. That is the basis of everything that follows.

That is the principle we must reassert today. It is our road back to constitutional government.

For many years, politicians have worked around aspects of the Constitution for short-term reasons. Now, We the People must give it new life.

In keeping with the Constitution, I pledge the following:

—As your president, I will not send American men and women to armed conflict without a congressional declaration of war. The last time the United States followed this constitutional requirement was more than seventy years ago. Is it a coincidence that our wars have not been as effective since that time? Let's return to the Constitution.

—I will submit international treaties to the Senate for the two-thirds vote required in the Constitution.

—I will strive to remove the special privileges that have been seized by the two dominant political parties. The Constitution does not provide for the duopoly of power amassed by the Democrats and Republicans. The legacy parties limit competition in various ways. Gerrymandering of congressional districts, for example, enables politicians to select their voters, rather than voters selecting their politicians.

—I will enforce the laws without fear or favor. When I took the oath of office, I swore to "take care that the laws are faithfully executed." When it comes to law enforcement, it should not matter who the president is. Elections should not decide which laws are enforced.

To this end, our laws and regulations must be dramatically simplified and reduced. Hard-working Americans should not have to fear lawsuits or bureaucratic meddling when going about their daily lives in an ethical, common-sense manner.

And make no mistake: complex laws and regulations are the handmaidens of special interests. Simplicity means accountability and fairness.

Ensure that Public Officials Live Under the Same Laws as Other Americans

Those entrusted to make or enforce the laws should live under the same laws as every other American.

That is so obvious. Regrettably, it's all too often been forgotten in Washington.

Our politicians and other officials often enjoy privileges that are altogether unjustified. By setting themselves apart, they are corrupting the institutions of government. Americans are entirely correct in being concerned when the counties surrounding Washington, DC have suddenly become the wealthiest in our nation.

In keeping with the Constitution, I pledge the following:

—As your president, I will seek abolition of the pension for ex-presidents. As a start, I will decline my right to a presidential pension.

—I will seek abolition of pensions for members of Congress.

—I will ask Congress to enact legislation repealing the so-called the full-time Congress. We will return to the constitutional vision of a Citizen Congress. Being a politician need no longer be their entire career.

They should spend more time in their districts, serving their constituents. In the twenty-first century, with communication and collaboration technology, there is no reason they should be nestled among special interests in the capital. Given that Congress is in session for approximately two days per week, this will also provide greater value for taxpayers.

Much of the time spent by representatives in Washington is fundraising for their next campaign. To turn their attention to the people's business, I will seek legislation banning fundraising while Congress is in session.

—I will direct that the civil service be updated for the twenty-first century. The benefits and incentives for public employees should be brought into line with other Americans. The "good enough for government work" ethic must be replaced by an ethic of public service. Every citizen should demand that public employees perform an honest day's work for an honest day's pay.

—I will ask Congress to update so-called "sovereign immunity" laws. These are old rules that prevent citizens from seeking redress against government failures. Going forward, when, for example, the Environmental Protection Agency pollutes a river—or lets down an entire city such as Flint, Michigan—it should face consequences just as severe as would private companies.

Update Public Institutions

President Reagan used to say, "The nearest thing to eternal life we will ever see on this earth is a government program."

Truer words were never spoken. The federal government is an agglomeration of complex, overlapping, unaccountable entities. They often have a life of their own, disconnected from the citizens they're meant to serve. In many cases, they are under the undue influence of special interests. Some agencies have become special interests unto themselves, impervious to effective oversight.

They're simply not serving the public.

In keeping with the Constitution, I pledge the following:

—As your president, I will bring together the best minds to create a commission to reorganize the federal government. This will be modelled on the Hoover Commission of the mid-twentieth century.

I will direct the commission to come up with recommendations on a strict deadline of one year.

Second, this commission will include members of Congress. They will be tasked with ensuring that any executive branch reorganization be linked with corresponding changes in relevant congressional committees. Otherwise, special interests might simply go to Congress to forestall executive branch reorganization.

—I will also direct that federal agencies undertake immediate steps to relocate civilian personnel from Washington. In our digital age, there's no reason why the government requires such a heavy footprint in the capital. Accordingly, we will disperse agencies across the country. This will bring public employees—your employees—closer to those they serve. It will also move them out of proximity to Washington lobbyists. This can also bring much-needed jobs and associated economic activity to areas that need them most.

Government Will Be Transparent

Every recent administration has committed to transparency. None have delivered.

Transparency is a key element of effective, twenty-first-century governance. If it is comprehensive and timely, it enables citizens to participate in the making of laws. There may have been a time when information and knowledge was centralized in Washington. In our Internet age, that is certainly not the case. There is a lot more wisdom, information, creativity and innovation outside of the capital than within it.

—As your president, I commit to making transparency a top priority. Except for circumstances protecting national security or privacy, the working assumption of your government should be transparency.

—I will work with Congress to ensure that all proposed legislation is made available online. This will be done with sufficient time for citizens to have meaningful input.

—I will give special attention to trade agreements. The secrecy of international trade negotiations has not served the American people in recent decades. Special interests have run riot. Going forward, trade deals will be open to citizen input throughout.

—Transparency must reach into the financing of political campaigns. "Dark money," campaign funds whose sources are hidden, can be corrupting. It disempowers citizens from informed evaluation of their government. Such transparency will include immediate Internet access to pertinent information. To make a meaningful difference, such reform must include political activities of not-for-profit organizations. All too often, foundations have become money laundering operations for politicians and the special interests they promote.

Looking Ahead

These reforms, taken together, would disrupt politics. All of them can be undertaken now. They do not require constitutional amendments. They are consistent with our constitutional system, as intended by our founders.

We the People would restore our rightful place as sovereigns of our government.

The extraordinary wisdom, creativity, energy and goodness of the American people could be aided, rather than handicapped, by our government.

The enduring values of the Constitution would be given new life, applying twenty-first century communication and collaboration.

As George Washington said of the Constitution in 1787: "I do not conceive that we are more inspired—have more wisdom—or possess more virtue than those who will come after us. The power under the Constitution will always be with the people."

And, as long as the power is with the people, the American future is bright.

The book that follows presents the case for why such extensive reform is urgent. It lays detailed rationales for the reforms mentioned in this draft speech, as well as many more proposals.

I would welcome hearing your ideas and reactions. This book is intended to stimulate thinking and action. Please connect via my website: servetolead.org.

—James Strock

Preface

Nearly everyone, everywhere—outside of Washington, DC—is having similar thoughts: *What is to be done to put our country back on track?*

The fact that you're taking the time to read these lines suggests that you, too, share such concerns.

What can any one person do? Alone…not so much. But, if one can help motivate others to bring their talents and dedication to bear, perhaps there's value in trying.

This brief book is my attempt to serve. It's not offered with the prideful sense that I have the answers. It's intended to fill a gap. My observation is that those who comprehend the realities of the Special Interest State tend to support the status quo. At the same time, those who recognize our governance crisis tend not to be schooled in the details necessary to achieve thoroughgoing reform.

I searched for a book that would meet this need. Not finding it, I determined to write it.

Ideally, this book might add value in helping point toward the right questions. If so, then the answers might follow, inspired and informed by the experience, wisdom, and practical idealism of many others. The end result, in the best American spirit, might extend far beyond what any of us might have imagined.

In, But Not Of

To borrow the evocative Christian phrase, my career has been in, but not of, politics and government.

I have spent approximately half of my career serving in government in various capacities. The roles have been diverse: federal and state; legislative and executive; political and administrative. The common thread is being tasked with challenging the status quo. I have always been an outsider, even when inside the process.

The other half of my career has been in the private sector. This has afforded me additional perspectives.

I've witnessed or participated as government has successfully undertaken great enterprises. These range from military actions to advancing environmental protection. I've seen and studied great leaders in government and politics, as well as in business, finance, and the not-for-profit sector.

The dawn of the twenty-first century is notable for the extraordinary disruption and progress that is remaking our lives and work. There are untold opportunities for leadership and service for individuals and networks and organizations.

At the same time, our government institutions are isolated and inert. Our office holders are captive to outdated and unsustainable patterns of thought and action.

Our government's dysfunction is disserving us. It's not merely a lost opportunity; it is impeding our progress. For the time being, with much of the rest of the world in even worse shape, mediocrity might seem sufficient. But it's not. If there's one thing we know, it's that disruption is coming. Other nations will move into whatever space we leave open for their aspiration and assertion.

That is just what the United States did during our turn as a rising power.

Don't Blame the Politicians

The United States faced challenges at the turn of the twentieth century every bit as profound as those at the turn of the twenty-first century.

One of the great leaders of that time, Theodore Roosevelt, declared:

"Sometimes I hear our countrymen…abroad saying: 'Oh, you mustn't judge us by our politicians...' I always want to interrupt and answer: 'You *must* judge us by our politicians.'"

Reformers are romanticized in retrospect. The reality is that those who break new paths are, necessarily, a bit rough around the edges. They're prone to be passionate. They may throw an elbow now and again. They're certain to make mistakes.

By definition, they're undertaking experiments. Sometimes they will succeed; far more often they will fall short. One thing is assured: those who strive to see and speak for the future will encounter the unremitting hostility of those satisfied with the status quo.

At the turn of the twenty-first century, our challenges once again call upon the sterner virtues. We must resist joining the ranks of the comfortable and complacent who reliably rationalize inaction.

Roosevelt harbored a visceral distaste for those he termed "the timid good." Such people might avoid doing wrong. Their personal conduct might be beyond reproach. Nonetheless, they might fall prey to pride, looking down their noses at those who err, who fall short—including their contemporaries actively contending in the great issues of their time. They might well be "content…with the negative merit of keeping [their] talents undamaged in a napkin." In the words of the poet Robert Browning, they're "faultless to a fault."

Seeing the challenge from another angle, the English writer Horace Walpole observed: "No country was ever saved by good men, because good men will not go to the length that may be necessary."

The people who forged our nation—and those who have advanced it in succeeding generations—overcame such self-indulgent inhibitions.

Throughout American history, some generations have been challenged to return to fundamentals. The times choose us. In a remarkable letter between two great Americans of the founding generation, John Adams wrote to his wife, Abigail:

> I must study politics and war that my sons may have liberty to study mathematics and philosophy. My sons ought to study mathematics and philosophy, geography, natural history, naval architecture, navigation, commerce, and agriculture, in order to give their children a right to study painting, poetry, music, architecture, statuary, tapestry, and porcelain.

After the initial battles are won, reformers will be succeeded by experts of polish and pedigree. People in elegant suits and paneled suites can elaborate and refine and routinize the arrangements of a new order. The best minds, the restless spirits can be freed, redirected to art and culture and private pursuits.

A Future So Bright We Need Sunglasses

Perhaps it's inevitable: some of those who recognize the need for major reform are pessimistic about the future. In some cases, it likely reflects their temperament. Others may fall prey to misleading simplicity, extrapolating negative trends into the future.

The naysayers are wrong. As John F. Kennedy was fond of saying, no one gets rich betting against the United States of America. If you want to renew your faith today, just glance at the energy and passion and creativity of millennials.

Given the spectacular leadership failures of recent decades, many young people, up to the middle aged, have not experienced government as a positive force. Some may have studied the history of presidents who provided Hamiltonian "energy in the executive," but they've not lived it.

Many of the ideas and observations in this book draw upon the lessons of prior generations. Such history is not offered for amusement or academic interest. It is intended to help link the immense potential of rising generations with the timeless lessons and values of our predecessors. Their visions and institutions are our unearned birthright—and our unavoidable responsibility.

As a young man in a family of longstanding achievement, Theodore Roosevelt saw the past as a blessing and a burden. His spirit was stirred by lines from Browning's "The Flight of the Duchess":

> All that the old Dukes had been, without knowing it,
> This Duke would fain know he was, without being it…

We are the beneficiaries of a precious, hard-earned legacy of constitutional government. Cutting through the complexity, the ultimate question is: Will we advance it, protect it, pass it along enlarged and enduring to future generations?

Every generation gets the history it deserves.

Now it's our turn.

The Consummation of Empire by Thomas Cole, 1836

Prelude

The Next American Century

We are living at an extraordinary moment. Consider some indicators:

- Harvard anthropologist Steven Pinker declares: "We may be living in the most peaceable era in the existence of our species." He speaks of the "New Peace." In the past thirty years, "organized conflicts of all kinds—civil wars, genocides, repression by autocratic governments, terrorist attacks—have declined throughout the world, and their death tolls have declined even more precipitously."
- The National Institute on Aging, part of the National Institutes of Health, declares: "The dramatic increase in average life expectancy during the 20th century ranks as one of society's greatest achievements. Although most babies born in 1900 did not live past age 50, life expectancy at birth now exceeds 83 years in Japan—the current leader—and is at least

81 years in several other countries." Looking ahead, "The global number of centenarians is projected to increase 10-fold between 2010 and 2050."

- Nobel laureate and Princeton economist Angus Deaton, referring to World Bank data, notes that the number of poor people, worldwide, living on less than a dollar per day, declined by at least three-quarters of a billion since 1981. This spectacular progress occurred even as the population of poor countries rose by approximately two billion people. He reports: "The fraction of the world's population that lives below a dollar a day has fallen from more than 40 percent to 14 percent." In sum: "Life is better now than at almost any time in history. More people are richer and fewer people live in dire poverty. Lives are longer and parents no longer routinely watch a quarter of their children die."
- The world is interconnected as never before. According to Internet World Stats, close to one-half of the global population is online. Facebook founder Mark Zuckerberg is spearheading a United Nations initiative to provide universal Internet connectivity by 2020. This will unlock untold value through education, distributed energy, and so much more.
- Transparency, combined with the capacity of individuals to publish writing and photographs online, is shifting the balance of power away from longstanding, centralized institutions. It's also affixing accountability. It's difficult to imagine that the industrialized genocides of the twentieth century—including the bloody handiwork of Hitler, Stalin, Mao, Pol Pot, and other infamous tyrants—could emerge outside of our line of vision today.

- The leaders of the twenty-first-century can serve as never before. One young woman, Malala Yousafzai, represents the future. Born in 1997, she was determined to obtain an education in her native Pakistan. To break her defiance and efface her example, a Taliban gunman shot her in the head. Malala—as she is now known universally—not only survived, but prevails. She is, without question, the first individual to be called out of her high school class to receive notice of being awarded the Nobel Peace Prize.

America is the source or center of many of these positive trends. Our values of freedom and self-expression and service are evolving in real time. We remain a magnet for talent. Americans are instigating disruption in many fields. Companies that did not exist a generation ago are creating immense value.

In 2016, the ten highest-valued companies in the world are American. So, too, the top twenty of the world's most valuable brands are dominated by American enterprises.

The era of General Motors and US Steel and Zenith Electronics and National Sugar Refining is giving way to the rise of Apple and Amazon and Facebook and Uber. The age of centralized institutions is receding amid an entrepreneurial insurgency.

In the United States, individuals are demanding—and achieving—ever greater freedom to express and advance our values through our lives and work. The deadening conformity endured by twentieth-century assembly-line workers and their white-collar counterparts in gray flannel suits is being supplanted by the twenty-first-century age of the entrepreneur.

According to the Kelly Group, approximately one-third of American workers self-identify as "free agents." This includes "independent contractors, freelance business owners, temporary employees," and "hybrids" who combine traditional employment with "gigs." The Kelly Group summarizes: "Free agents are confident of their value. They don't live to work. They organize their work around their lives."

We're also expressing our values as consumers. More and more companies are learning that advancing customers' values creates value. Enterprises that historically devalued environmental-social-governance issues are striving to make them part of their brands. Companies that violate our trust are more likely to be called out and penalized in the marketplace.

American ingenuity is achieving breakthroughs in medicine and public health. Not only is science advancing, but so are the means of distribution around the world. From the Gates Foundation through a multitude of other organizations, people in need are served as never before.

Longstanding logjams are breaking, with new laws expanding personal autonomy. Same-sex marriage has become a reality. Rights of self-determination at the end of life are being recognized.

Trends are positive for high-profile social issues. Abortion rates are down. Divorce rates are down. Violent crime rates are down.

Amid this ferment of freedom, our values are resonating around the world. Our cultural offerings find audiences everywhere, most notably among the young.

As the world staggered toward war in 1941, *Time* publisher Henry Luce proclaimed "the American century."

The legendary leader of modern Singapore, Lee Kuan Yew, looked ahead during a visit to China in 2005. According to an American who was present, Lee sought to disabuse rising Chinese triumphalism: "I have news for you. The twenty-first century will be America's century, too. Americans have an extraordinary capacity to reinvent themselves, to learn from their mistakes, and to innovate. Don't underestimate them."

Paradox of Success

We face a paradox of our success. Other nations are adopting traditional American virtues of hard work, thrift, and investment in the future. As a result, they are rising by various indicators. In a world shaped by American values, they see a future worth fighting for.

Paradoxically, facing the same circumstances from a different perspective, many Americans lack confidence in our national future.

Poll after poll finds Americans gripped by an uncharacteristic pessimism. Many of us no longer have faith that our children will achieve better lives.

There is widespread dissatisfaction with our governing institutions. Congress languishes. Presidents fail to command respect. Citizens stream out of the two-party system. According to the Gallup Poll, a plurality of Americans now declares themselves independents. In many elections, voter participation is at all-time lows.

Perhaps most evocative of our moment, many Americans—perhaps a majority—regard their government with anxiety if not fear. According to the Gallup polling organization in 2015:

> Almost half of Americans, 49%, say the federal government poses "an immediate threat to the rights and freedoms of ordinary citizens," similar to what was found in previous surveys conducted over the last five years. When this question was first asked in 2003, less than a third of Americans held this attitude.

As Lincoln reminded us, our government derives its legitimacy solely from the consent of the governed. It exists to serve us. It acts in our name.

Our lingering anomie is a significant development that demands our undivided attention.

Is America in Decline?

Unsurprisingly, such public sentiments coalesce into an overarching concern: *Is America in decline?*

When did this unsettling thought first flash through your mind?

Perhaps it was when the top priority of the American government in 2013—health insurance reform—exploded on takeoff.

The greatest nation on earth was belatedly attempting to upgrade its notoriously troubled health-care sector. The fundamental promise used to secure its passage—*if you like your current plan, you can keep it*—was discarded by proponents without a pretense of remorse. Long-overdue reforms—such as overriding insurance company limits on pre-existing conditions—were freighted with an incomprehensible mass of special-interest provisions that were concealed prior to enactment. Many Americans conclude that the net result is worse than before.

Perhaps it was when you returned to your high school. If you're of a certain age, you might be shaken to discover how few students graduate—often less than half.

Perhaps it was when you reflected on the United States pouring lives and treasure into a series of far-away, preemptive wars in the post-9/11 world. There has been no declaration of war as stipulated in the Constitution. Two presidents, of different political parties, failed to present a clear understanding of what would constitute "victory." Successive congressional sessions, of various partisan alignments, failed to hold the administrations to account.

Without clarity at the beginning of the engagement, confusion has reigned throughout. No one knows when or where it will all end. Immense sacrifices are exacted from a startlingly small slice of the American people—the real "1 percenters," who carry the rest of us on their strong shoulders. In jarring contrast, our politicians are unable to summon the will to enact dedicated taxes to pay for the conflicts in which others' sons and daughters will sacrifice their lives and livelihoods.

Perhaps it was when you beheld American officials, donning the ill-fitting cloak of imperial presumption, flying haplessly from capital to capital, earnestly presuming to midwife lasting national borders in the Middle East.

All the while, the southern border of the United States is sundered, decade after decade, in calculated chaos created in Washington. Franklin Roosevelt and an earlier generation of American politicians controlled immigration to enable the welfare state to take hold. Today, our ever-expanding web of transfer programs, already manifestly unsustainable, has become a de facto safety valve for the failed governance of other nations.

Paradoxically, as the number of noncitizens resident in the United States has risen and become entrenched, it is easy to lose sight of its practical significance. The projected number of those illegally present at times approaches the number of unemployed American citizens. Bereft of the full protections of American citizens, undocumented immigrants are condemned to live in the shadows, vulnerable to those who prey upon them, ranging from unscrupulous employers to ruthless criminal gangs.

Meanwhile, highly skilled, prospective immigrants from around the world are discouraged by inexplicably inhospitable legal hurdles.

Perhaps you've encountered the failures of government to achieve basic infrastructure tasks. Every community has its stories.

For example, the San Francisco–Oakland Bay Bridge was retrofitted—more than two decades after the Loma Prieta earthquake of 1989. As politicians indulged their familiar rituals of self-celebration, routine engineering reviews located widespread structural defects. By comparison, the Golden Gate Bridge was constructed in just four years, beginning in 1933. Or, consider the billion-dollar companies that have risen in the Bay Area in the past decade.

Perhaps it was when you observed the abject failures of government—even under presidential direction—to respond effectively to the devastation wrought by Hurricane Katrina.

Perhaps it was when you witnessed or experienced the casual incompetence and inert thought processes of government officials. Flash back to Katrina and the bumbling presidential appointees, confirmed by the Senate. Think of your recent visit to your local US Postal Service office, where many employees are more concerned about serving their unionized management than the citizens who pay their salaries. Think of your telephone call to the Internal Revenue Service, whereby you enter a parallel universe of long wait times, repeated redirections, and no final answers.

Perhaps your contact with the IRS was even more damaging. Have you been on one of their political hit lists?

Perhaps it was when you learned that the National Security Agency has undertaken unprecedented undercover data gathering from millions of American citizens.

Perhaps it was when you realized that the greatest beacon of freedom in history has transformed itself, improbably, into the greatest jailer on Earth.

Perhaps it was when you beheld the totality of the politicization of American law enforcement. That massive prison population has some conspicuous absentees.

Privileged firms and individuals are presumed protected. In the notorious financial debacle that culminated in the crash of 2008, systematized legerdemain profited exorbitantly. Legatees of historic financial houses liquidated decades of accumulated public trust for immediate enrichment. Nonetheless, not one high-level Wall Street executive was indicted or convicted of corporate crime. Even the former chair of the Federal Reserve, Ben Bernanke, has publicly regretted this result.

While Wall Street grips Washington in a stranglehold, New York's finest, armed for warfare, forced a fatal, fateful chokehold on a gentle man of the street. His tragic death was caught indelibly on camera.

No indictments issued. Eric Garner's alleged crime: selling loose cigarettes.

Perhaps there's no greater breach of faith with the future than the endless tides of debt washing across every aspect of our national life.

Public debt is astronomical. It took two centuries for the United States to incur our first trillion dollars of national debt. In the Bush-Obama years, it rose from $5.8 trillion in 2001, hurtling inexorably toward $20 trillion.

Standard & Poor's downgraded the sovereign credit rating of the United States. Not long ago, this would have been unthinkable. In the event, our politicians conspired to render it unmentionable. Rather than attack the problem, members of the administration attacked the rating agency.

Ominously, when the European Union sought outside investment to alleviate its debt crisis, it turned to the new national banker on the world scene: China.

Unlike the national government, state and local government entities cannot obscure reality amid an avalanche of printed money.

Nonetheless, they have their own ways to evade fiscal accountability. For decades, politicians who were foreclosed from tax increases have turned to innovative, nontransparent ways to incur debt. Grotesquely underfunded public employee pensions are a rising plague on numerous cities, counties, and states. Failed cities appear as apparitions of an unwelcome future. A grim milestone was passed when the historic city of Detroit declared bankruptcy. Will other cities—even states—follow?

Public officials and Wall Street share a defining fiduciary obligation: they're entrusted with other people's money. More and more, they're not simply spending other people's money—they're spending our children's money. Even our children's children's money.

Outsiders—such as the generations who survived the Great Depression of the 1930s—might well be gobsmacked by the ongoing ensnarement of young people into debt. Rising generations are steeped in a toxic ecosystem of debt and entitlement. They are subject to an unprecedented social experiment of state-of-the-art, 24/7 consumerism. Many of their parents—some for good reason, others not—live relentlessly beyond their means.

Subsidized student loans have emerged as a gateway to adult status in the debt culture. Young people are conditioned to believe that a college education is invariably a wise investment. They run up staggering loans that they have no context to comprehend.

Millennials enter the global marketplace, weighted with rocks in their rucksacks: more than $30,000 in average student loan debt.

Where are the historic congressional hearings that hold educational administrators and lending institutions to account for their enabling, self-interested complicity in this vast enrichment scheme? Instead, our politicians assert their generosity, piously propping up the status quo, offering plans for debt forgiveness for our graduates. Who can doubt that the ultimate result will be passing yet more debt to generations yet to be born?

It's not enough for the older generations to bequeath debt. They're also sitting atop a political system that transfers immense wealth from the young through health and social security entitlements.

As dangerous as the financial debt burden can be for future generations, it's at least capable of reliable quantification. Not so for our environmental debts. Egregiously, the United States has heedlessly led the world into an uncontrolled experiment: How much carbon dioxide can be emitted into the atmosphere, at what risk? No one can know the prospective costs this may entail for rising generations.

For generations in power to tie the hands of their successors with such debts is the essence of selfishness and irresponsibility. For a nation whose government is based on consent of the governed, it's a travesty. All the more when we consider how the generations now in power benefitted from incalculable advantages granted by the sacrifices of our forebears.

Governance Failure

When one steps back, one recognizes opposing trends:

- The American people are serving the world in untold ways, changing things for the better. The impact of our actions, including the influence of our example, is transformative.
- At the same time, our governance is failing to rise to the level of events.

Government is supposed to enable us to achieve important tasks that otherwise would be impossible. Recall great projects from the American past: construction of the Panama Canal; our transformation into the "arsenal of democracy" in the Second World War; the development of our water and highway systems; the moon shot.

It would be troubling enough if our governance failures were simply robbing us of our potential. The reality is even worse: our dysfunctional government is metastasizing into a lethal threat to our continued progress and preeminence.

The front line of our governance is our politics. It's where we express our values and transform them into unified decisions and actions.

Increasingly, elections fail to align government with citizens' expressed values.

Politicians of one of the legacy parties, then the other, take the stage promising change. All too often, the changes they have in mind appear to be more significant for them than for the rest of us.

An unmistakable, circular process has emerged. Limited to only two choices, more and more of us vote against the party in power. We vote out the Republicans in one election. Newly elected Democrats misread the result—and seek to advance the agenda of their special-interest coalition. In turn, we vote out the Democrats. Newly elected Republicans misread the result—and seek to advance the agenda of their special-interest coalition.

Historic milestones, such as China's becoming the world's largest economy in 2014, go unremarked. Universally recognized areas of government failure remain unaddressed.

It is apparently not enough that the legacy parties are deadlocked in a reactionary embrace. We shift in our seats uneasily as Democrats take victory laps for their undoubted accomplishments from the 1960s. The Republicans do the same for the 1980s. No longer content to offer ideas from a vanished world, they also turn to politicians from the past.

Moving toward the 2016 national elections, many partisans saw no problem in putting forward yet another Bush and yet another

Clinton as adequate for this historic moment. It is not inapt to wonder if we've been gaslighted in a long-playing, abusive relationship.

The American founders fought to displace the aristocracy that was grinding down our freedom and potential. From a population under three million, they summoned extraordinary talent to the task. That fold in time is memorable for the leadership of George Washington, John Adams, James Madison, Alexander Hamilton, Thomas Jefferson, and Benjamin Franklin. Equally important are the sacrifices of many, many others who placed their lives, limbs, and treasure on the line for the idea of a nation built on the aspirations of the Declaration of Independence.

At the dawn of the twenty-first century, the American nation comprises 320 million people. We command resources and power that the most visionary of the founders could scarcely contemplate.

All too often, we treat this trust cavalierly, as if we are entitled to our privileged position. We regard it as the natural order of things.

At the same time, we sense that our present circumstances cannot hold. Our politics, far from providing a compass or a map, has declined into a clamorous distraction.

Like a ghost ship holding untold riches from a storied past, America is adrift in uncharted waters, heedless of storm warnings.

All the while, pious pundits, professors, and politicians stroke their chins, tsk-tsking the citizens who are, increasingly, declining to participate in our broken governance.

Reality Check

For all these challenges, is there any nation in the world with whom we would wish to change places?

Certainly not.

Amid our largely self-created travails, the world continues to look to America for leadership. For the time being, the absence of alternatives obscures our precarious circumstances. International investment has poured into our stock and real estate markets, supercharged by the "easy money" policies of the Federal Reserve and other central banks.

Some, focusing on past glories, pine wistfully for the US preeminence of the post–World War II moment.

That is a vanished world. The American Century, as recognized by Henry Luce, is over.

Nonetheless, Lee Kuan Yew's optimism is better placed than our national mood of debilitating despair. If you seek tangible evidence relating to our greatest emerging competitor, consider the staggering sums of Chinese capital moving into the United States.

It is within our reach to render the twenty-first century a new American Century.

As with so much else, Winston Churchill foresaw our potential. In the midst of the Second World War, on September 6, 1943, he spoke at Harvard of the world that could emerge with the ultimate victory. He envisioned science making possible unprecedented mobility and interconnections among peoples. Churchill concluded: "Such plans offer far better prizes than taking away other people's provinces or lands or grinding them down in exploitation. *The empires of the future are the empires of the mind."* [emphasis added]

Will we seize this opportunity? Will we evolve from twentieth-century constructs of dominance and dictation toward our twenty-first-century comparative advantages of influence and example?

For the moment, amid all our national challenges, we retain a priceless gift from prior generations: to an extraordinary extent, we control our own destiny.

For the moment. Nations, like individuals, confront a stern decree: What's taken for granted will be taken away.

To preserve and enlarge our hard-earned historic legacy, we must reform our national government. To reform our government, we must change our politics.

To change our politics, We the People must assert our leadership.

If Not Us, Who?

A public-spirited and accomplished person recently said to me:

> I don't think there's much to be done about the breakdown of the country. What difference can I make? I've voted for the Democrats, I've voted for the Republicans...*but nothing changes.* Washington is impervious to repair, as best I can tell...I'm just focused on looking after my children and grandchildren, doing whatever I can to make their lives as good as possible...I'm not optimistic about their future... Rome went down, Britain went down, now America's going down...

This is a comprehensible—if not particularly admirable—response for an individual. Not everyone is expected to sign up for the arduous task of national reconstruction, at least in the political realm.

What may be excusable for an individual can be devastating if it comes to represent an accepted, declining standard of citizenship.

One senses that defeatist sentiments are spreading. Millions of Americans can't be bothered to cast a vote—and it's not difficult to do, by any historical standard. Vast numbers believe that America is "on the wrong track." Polls suggest that a third of Americans would entertain abandoning their homeland, repatriating.

A democratic republic is not sustainable if rising numbers among us wring our hands over the whole situation. If anything could be aptly dismissed with the epithet "un-American," it would be such self-indulgent fatalism.

Our challenges are interwoven. There is a need to comprehend and face the facts before us. There is a need to raise our national character to that of "the greatest generation" of the World War II era (and other great American generations, from the Revolution, through the Civil War, through the Progressive Era, and the Cold War).

Reform of our political institutions is essential to this process. If our politics can be returned to serving our people, a positive feedback loop between our political system and the national character can propel us forward.

Twenty-first-century American government can be reconceived, reinvented. It can become a platform on which Americans can create "apps" that effectively serve current and future generations—and the world.

Contrary to common understanding in some elite quarters, our constitutional framework is not the problem. By a stroke of fate, it's arguably more relevant to our current challenges than it was a century ago.

Disrupt Politics—With a Roadmap

This manifesto has three parts:

The Great Reckoning. This section outlines a series of ongoing, unaddressed challenges confronting the United States. Presidents and Congresses controlled by Democrats and Republicans, in various configurations, have failed to frame or resolve consequential issues over the course of a generation.

The ongoing governance failures are so significant as to render our way of life unsustainable.

By now it's clear that the status quo in Washington, DC, cannot be expected to rise to the level of events of our time. A number of issues—some recognized as fundamental, others as divisive but diversionary—have festered for decades.

As Harvard Law School professor Larry Lessig persuasively argues, if we are intent on fulfilling our unfinished agenda, *we must fix democracy first.*

A Great Reckoning is coming. The question is: On whose terms will it occur? Will the generations of Americans now holding power take decisive action to bring about change? Or will we join the ranks of all insolvent debtors, abandoning our fate to the whims of creditors?

The Special Interest State. The disquieting continuity of the Bush-Obama years points to a sobering conclusion: *Our top officials are products of, and are presiding over, a system.*

Presidents Barack Obama and George W. Bush are very different individuals. Their partisans see them as polar opposites.

Nonetheless, when one dispassionately examines the record, their administrations are of a piece. The continuities are so striking that only diehard, myopic partisans can overlook them. As a European friend declared: If you gazed upon the United States from a distance, you might well assume that the Bush-Obama years were a single, overlong administration.

The operations of the executive and legislative branches are objectively dysfunctional (which inevitably means that the judiciary is also off course). Public opinion polls find a widespread sense that our public institutions are riddled with corruption.

Nonetheless, the failure of official governance should not incline us toward a comforting misperception that there's not a *system* at work. It merely means that the *actual* system is not recognized for what it is, for what it does.

That system is the *Special Interest State.* It is working well—for those it is serving. It's bigger than the Democrats and the Republicans. It's succeeding as the government fails. Its capture of the White House and Congress is so thoroughgoing that its totality is easy to overlook.

Current and recent occupants of the White House and Congress, being products of this system, cannot see it for what it is (or, if they do stumble upon this truth, they pick themselves up, brush themselves off, and move smartly along). Spoiler alert: Just as our parents were slow to back off from their explanations that babies come from the stork, the powers that be do not want us to see how our political class came to be.

We will get into the earthy, often unpleasant details of how the Special Interest State operates, how it perpetuates itself. To diagnose the problem properly is the necessary first step to curing it.

Today's Washington can best be comprehended as a self-serving, self-sustaining system—*of the special interests, by the special interests, for the special interests.*

The early indications are that the selection process for the third presidential administration of the twenty-first century will perpetuate the status quo. This brings to mind Auric Goldfinger's admonition to James Bond: "Once is happenstance. Twice is coincidence. The third time it's enemy action."

A Twenty-First-Century Declaration of Independence. Once one recognizes the extent of the challenges, one might well be paralyzed into inaction. Many recent proposals for change are so unworkable as to be nonstarters.

For example, there are increasing calls for constitutional amendments to recast our institutional arrangements. Some even seek a new constitutional convention.

The Constitution includes provisions for amendments that are as essential as any other provisions. The challenge is, the amendment process is tortuous.

Focusing on constitutional change may also miss a larger point.

Many of the dysfunctions we labor under are not so much the result of the Constitution. Rather, they arose from work-arounds by twentieth-century politicians.

Fortunately, the ideals of the Declaration of Independence, pursued through the institutions of the Constitution, remain highly relevant for our time.

Could any scaffolding of governance be better suited for a vast, diverse, twenty-first-century nation? The ongoing disruption of our time—decentralizing information, decentralizing power, creating value through accelerating accountability and ad hoc organizational arrangements—is making old notions new again.

The Special Interest State has emerged as a formidable obstacle to change. Twentieth-century, centralized governmental institutions and assumptions are being sustained long past their sell-by date by political enterprises making use of twenty-first-century social media and digital tools.

This baleful paradox cannot stand forever. Our governmental structures and customs remain in a rearguard action against the technologically based disruption that has touched nearly every other part of American life and work.

We need a twenty-first-century Declaration of Independence from the Special Interest State.

The principles and proposals offered here do not depend on chimerical notions of constitutional amendments and conventions.

Nonetheless, they would profoundly change the way Washington works. They're based on citizens and communities and states retrieving power and prerogatives that they have reposed in the federal government over the course of the twentieth century.

The operating system of our government, the Constitution, has been corrupted by an accretion of opportunistic alterations. Our task is to restore and refresh that operating system.

It's not necessary that we possess the wisdom or courage or sacrifice of the founders. Nonetheless, it's a significant leadership task. It requires that we spur ourselves to action, rather than vainly wait for the Special Interest State to voluntarily relinquish its privileges.

If Not Now, When?

The year 2026 will be the 250th anniversary of the Declaration of Independence.

Thomas Jefferson is credited with the injunction that each generation needs a new revolution. Why not set 2026 as our deadline for declaring independence from the Special Interest State?

On July 4, 2026, will we be able to assert that our nation has met the promise of the founders? Or, will we have validated the doubters—then and now—and lost the republic?

The greatest generations of American history are revered because they summoned the ideals and actions to master existential challenges.

Will successor generations honor us for enabling them to make the twenty-first century a new American Century?

Disrupt Politics

Prelude

- The early twenty-first century represents an extraordinary, historic moment. The positive trends for health and well-being, worldwide, are unmistakable. The United States is the source and center of many of these achievements.
- Paradox of success: At the moment that many of our values are in global ascendancy, Americans are uncertain about our own prospects.
- There is an unmistakable failure of governance. People increasingly see our federal government as a negative—somewhere on the spectrum between an irrelevance and a threat.
- Much of our concern about the future is actually concern about our dysfunctional governance.
- We hold a precious legacy: To an extent rare in history, we have the capacity to determine our national future.
- To preserve this precious, hard-earned freedom, we must reform our national government. To reform our government, we must change our politics. To change our politics, We the People must assume the task of leadership.
- Aiming for the 250th anniversary of the Declaration of Independence in 2026, we can disrupt our politics. We can craft a twenty-first-century Declaration of Independence from the Special Interest State.

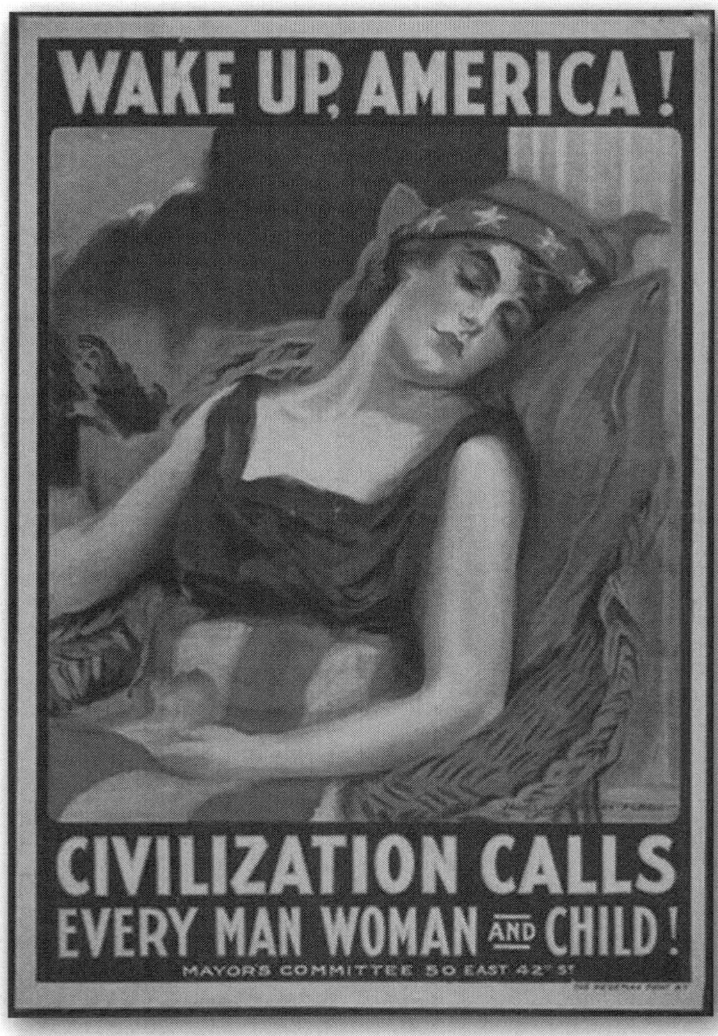

Wake Up America! by James Montgomery Flagg, 1916

One

The Great Reckoning

If something cannot go on forever, it will stop.

—Herbert Stein

The things that will destroy America are prosperity-at-any-price, peace-at-any-price, safety-first instead of duty-first, and love of soft living and the get-rich-quick theory of life.

—Theodore Roosevelt

To state the facts frankly is not to despair the future nor indict the past. The prudent heir takes careful inventory of his legacies and gives a faithful accounting to those whom he owes an obligation of trust.

—John F. Kennedy

In the years following the financial panic of 2008, there has been a lot of back and forth about how to label this historical moment. Are we in a Great Recession?

That term has wide currency, yet it is incomplete. There is an overarching sense that America's challenges are of a greater magnitude.

The crisis that afflicted us in 2008 goes beyond finance and economics. It's also political, governmental, cultural—and, perhaps, spiritual.

We're touched by an ubiquitous sense of foreboding. Things cannot go on as they are. Polls indicate that large majorities of the American people believe the nation is moving in the wrong direction.

There is manifest yearning for decisive, effective political leadership that rises to the level of events. Yet, when we look to Washington, DC, we're repeatedly disappointed.

Government cannot be expected to solve all of our problems. Yet its dysfunction can inhibit our capacity to achieve our potential.

For the time being, the status quo trundles along. We make great leaps of progress in some areas, while falling backward in others. Amid crowded hours, we rationalize averting our attention from hard choices and difficult tasks.

A Great Reckoning is coming: Will it be on our terms—or will it be imposed by others?

From the hard-earned sacrifices of earlier generations, we have the enviable capacity to determine our national fate. That freedom can also seem a burden. For the moment, no one is forcing our hand. There is no immediate, existential threat from war or another Great Depression or other such catastrophe.

There is, instead, an accumulation of smaller threats. None of them alone is sufficient to threaten our way of life. Yet, unaddressed, one or more may metastasize, with cataclysmic consequences.

The challenge is comparable to that of a patient with early-stage arteriosclerosis or diabetes. For a time, there is much that can be done. It is also possible to procrastinate without immediate consequences. The longer one defers action, the fewer options remain for full recovery—and the greater the risk of irreversible decline.

The issues that follow are each caused or exacerbated by long-standing failures of governance. It is unreasonable to suppose that any or all of them will be resolved without thoroughgoing reform of our government and politics.

Debt Culture

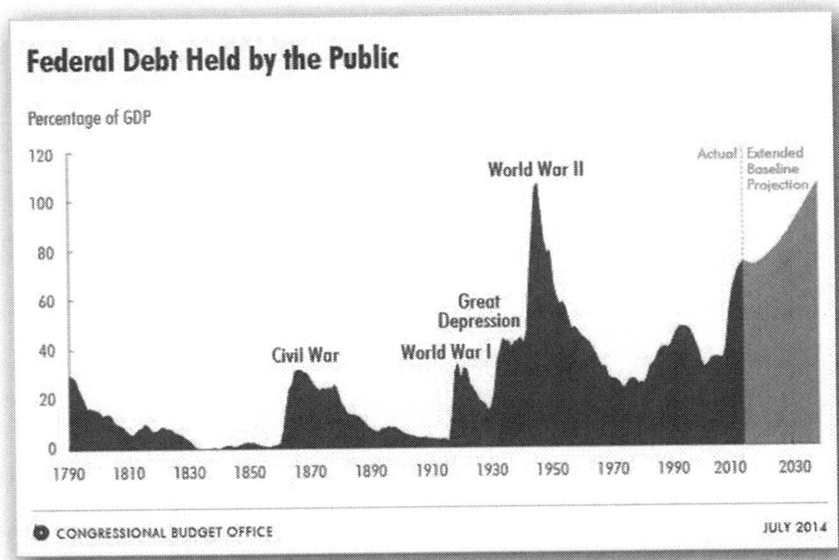

The American founders were profoundly conscious of the dangers of public debt. One of the triggers of our revolution was the high taxation exacted to sustain the British imperial war machine. Debt was seen as a threat to autonomy, for nations as for individuals. Even "good" debt—such as for infrastructure—was controversial in many quarters for much of our nation's early history.

Today we are in entirely different circumstances. Our national debt is soaring. Its magnitude is so great as to defy public comprehension.

The generations now holding power are ignoring our debts of honor to our predecessors, while imposing unprecedented debts on rising generations.

As Democrats and Republicans point their fingers at one another, the United States remains on a trajectory of ever-increasing long-term debt. The public debt rose to more than $19 trillion in 2016. It approached $20 trillion by the end of the Obama administration. By any pertinent measure—ratio of debt to gross domestic product or to tax revenue—this is an extraordinary number. Absent decisive action, it's going to get worse over the course of the coming decades. Ominously, there are many other federal government liabilities (such as Social Security Disability Insurance) that are not generally recognized or publicly discussed, much less being addressed.

Politicians routinely obfuscate the situation. Some conflate the year-to-year operating *deficits* of the federal government with the cumulative national *debt*. The annual deficits rise and fall. The accumulated debt inexorably rises.

In an era when resistance to higher taxes is hardening, politicians are less likely to be rewarded for directly shifting resources from one group of citizens to others through new programs. Their unspoken default is to finance current expenditures by incurring debt. As our founders might have said, for future generations this amounts to taxation without representation.

To be sure, incurring debt can be justified in some circumstances. For example, financing infrastructure can enable ongoing value creation. Debt for existential emergencies such as war or short-term stimulus can be necessary. On the other hand, incurring long-term debt for present consumption is intergenerational theft.

Our political officeholders feel constrained by ever fewer scruples in this respect. In some cases, presidents rationalize running up debt as constraining their successors' capacities to reorder their spending priorities. Thus conservatives and liberals overlook deficit spending by their favored administrations. Such self-serving arguments garnered passing plausibility in the past, when there was a broader consensus against incurring public debt. Today, it's not persuasive to presume that succeeding presidents will face political pressure to be more fiscally responsible. There is no group such as the AARP (formerly the American Association of Retired Persons) relentlessly defending the interests of future generations.

Politicians regard themselves as innovative if they discover previously untapped funds that can be plundered for current expenditure. For example, in 2015, President Obama acceded to a House Republican demand that the bankrupt Highway Trust Fund be rescued with $60 billion plundered from an entirely unrelated Federal Reserve banking program. Self-styled fiscally conservative politicians viewed this as preferable to increasing gasoline taxes to maintain a manifestly declining highway system.

The "trust" element of our highway funding has long since been violated by all manner of reallocations. Special interests run riot.

The trucking industry, in political alliance with their unions, applies political muscle to ensure that much of the cost imposed by their road use is collected from gasoline taxes on private vehicles. The heaviest users—in every sense—of our freeways are thereby subsidized by the rest of us.

The arrangement becomes hard to manage, because gas tax revenues from ordinary drivers are declining. Environmental policies have encouraged people to drive cleaner, more fuel-efficient vehicles, or use alternatives when available. The Highway Trust Fund therefore faces a funding crisis.

Amid the realpolitik of the budget bazaar, the politicians and their special-interest sponsors reached into an entirely unrelated program, raided the funds, and declared victory. Any twinges of conscience will likely be forgotten amid high-fives all around, from the White House to the Capitol. Special interests will fete their favored politicians with dinners and awards for their "public service." Campaign contributions will follow.

The loose ends remain to be tied up in the misty future. The next time the music stops, the various politicians, Democrats and Republicans alike, will have sorted themselves out in new chairs. Institutional memory will fade. Urgent reactions to the next budget crisis will further efface accountability and coherence. And the dance goes on.

Lowering the bar in Washington is followed by corresponding approaches in the states. State and local finances are all too often compromised by unsustainable debt obligations. Underfunded pensions are widespread. The bills are coming due. Things are getting real. Current services are squeezed as short-term financial expedients run out.

For example, in 2015, the governor of Arizona proposed spending down the principal of the state's land trust. The land trust is intended to provide a reliable, ongoing source of funding for education and other fundamental public needs. Like other conventional politicians, the governor seeks to apply proceeds of the savings of past generations to current spending—to the detriment of future generations.

A Democratic president and Republican Congress were co-conspirators in the highway fund legerdemain. In Arizona, the governor and legislative majorities were Republicans. Yet they were readily able to garner support for the trust fund raid from interest groups aligned with Democrats. Partisan divisions were overlooked in the rush to grab resources for current spending at the expense of future generations.

In Washington, the systemic corruption is so entrenched that many of the participants feel powerless to challenge it. Many are so accustomed to it that they may be desensitized to the problem. In the states, such institutional corruption is in plain sight. Cinderella's wicked stepsisters have nothing on the standard-issue politicians who proclaim themselves guardians of the young—while plundering their trust funds, which they are intended to protect.

Don't wait for the state politicians' consciences to be stirred. One might think that their proximity to the voters would hold them in check.

Think again. State and local politics and politicians are so uninspiring that many citizens just look the other way. Turnout is embarrassingly low in many elections. On budget issues, Democrats and Republicans alike suppress turnout to serve their special-interest masters. Rather than consolidating matters in general elections, they can overpower opposition in low-turnout special elections. Given the ease with which votes can be engineered in these off-season ballots, they might as well have truth in labelling: "special interest" elections.

Amid all this noise, something big is afoot. America is being transformed from a nation of savers to a nation of debtors. The Federal Reserve's unprecedented, multiyear experiment in artificially "easy money" reflects and spurs this unwelcome change. Savers, deprived of normal interest rates, are nudged toward debt or risky investment alternatives. Asset bubbles inflate and burst. Wall Street and wealthy individuals pocket handsome gains. Capital is misallocated. The virtues of saving being unrewarded, there is less reason to defer gratification for a better future.

Further government borrowing is encouraged by the lower costs of debt service. The prospect of normalized rates becomes terrifying for politicians. Washington and Wall Street, with the connivance of the Federal Reserve, join hands in deferring the reckoning.

The culture of debt can be seen more broadly. Significant environmental and public health risks are willfully ignored or understated. Infrastructure is not maintained, much less updated to world class standards. A banquet of consequences is being set for rising and future generations.

Prior generations of Americans took great pains to ensure that their successors would have more freedom through less indebtedness. That is our inheritance.

In recent decades, the laser focus on serving future generations has dissipated. All too often, their prospects are plundered for our comfort. It brings to mind the wry observation of George Bernard Shaw: "A government that robs Peter to pay Paul can always depend on the support of Paul."

The ever-increasing reliance on arrangements built on debt fuels a far-reaching hubris. Without fiscal discipline, decisions are avoided, elided, or deferred. There's an implicit assumption that resources are unlimited.

Our forebears might well wonder why we are not moving heaven and earth to bequeath more rather than less to future generations.

Outdated Revenue System

The year 2013 was the centenary of the modern American income tax system. The occasion was not marked by public celebrations. What was unexpected was the absence of discussion of updating and reforming a revenue system that is overdue for a twenty-first-century reset.

Prior to the enactment of the graduated income tax, the predominant source of federal government funding was a system of tariffs.

Special interests commandeered the political system, seeking protection or preferences. The inevitable result was widespread corruption, from the US Custom House in New York to the halls of power in Washington. Political reform was a powerful current in the rising tide of sentiment demanding a twentieth-century tax system.

Today's federal income tax regime reaches into all aspects of our national life. The system is complex beyond common understanding. *Fortune* magazine reported in 2015 that annual filing costs exceed $140 billion. The tax preparation industry is valued at more than $10 billion, with more than three hundred thousand employees.

One might suppose that such numbers—and the inefficiency they illuminate—would spur action in Washington, DC. Instead, for all its flaws, the tax structure is remarkably resistant to reform.

Every sentence of the thousands of pages of tax statutes and regulations is the handiwork of one special interest or another. It's not an accident that the Senate Finance Committee and House Ways and Means Committee are highly sought-after assignments for our solons. There's no better perch for raising funds for political campaigns.

The bias toward the status quo is striking. The current corporate tax structure is widely recognized as suboptimal. The nominal rates are high by international standards. Numerous industries have obtained preferential treatment through the political process. This adds considerable complexity and distorts the allocation of capital. Meanwhile, capital and talent are moving abroad in search of better treatment. Some high-profile American companies are reincorporating in other nations through "corporate inversions."

More broadly, as the United States encounters rising competition in global markets, there is little sustained examination of the pros and cons of resetting the revenue system from its reliance on taxing income toward taxing consumption.

Many economists, liberal and conservative, agree that carbon taxes hold promise as an element of a smart, twenty-first-century revenue system. They might be crafted to reduce payroll or income taxes. They could have a positive environmental impact, incenting investment in clean technologies. They might substitute for costly command-and-control regulations on motor vehicles and other industries.

Nonetheless, carbon taxes remain politically orphaned.

So it is with many areas of the tax system that are overdue for a new look. The last thoroughgoing reform was a generation ago, in 1986.

Whether one's priority is distribution of income and wealth, economic efficiency, international competitiveness, or otherwise, there is much to be done. Until the political system is repaired, it appears that the status quo will remain.

A Republic or an Empire?

A recurring theme throughout our history is the tension between our republican government and virtues and the temptations and demands of empire. In his Farewell Address in 1796, George Washington warned of "those overgrown military establishments, which under any form of government are inauspicious to liberty, and which are to be regarded as particularly hostile to republican liberty."

On the anniversary of the Declaration of Independence, July 4, 1821, Secretary of State John Quincy Adams elaborated on this understanding of America's unique role in the world:

> Wherever the standard of freedom and independence has been or shall be unfurled, there will her heart, her benedictions and her prayers be. But she goes not abroad, in search of monsters to destroy. She is the well-wisher to the freedom

> and independence of all. She is the champion and vindicator only of her own. She will commend the general cause, by the countenance of her voice, and the benignant sympathy of her example.

Given our history, we do not tend to refer to America's international role as imperial. Such a description conjures up visions of self-serving colonial approaches entirely at variance with our values. Nonetheless, by whatever name, the United States has come to define our interests as global.

Our national expenditures for defense are staggering. The National Priorities Project summarizes: for fiscal year 2015, spending for the Pentagon and related programs totals nearly $600 billion. This represents 54 percent of all federal "discretionary" spending (the part of the budget that is legislated through congressional appropriations). By contrast, "entitlement" programs, such as Social Security and Medicare, are automatically funded on a mandatory basis.

US military expenditures approach the combined total of the next seven largest military budgets in the world. The significance of this development is seen not only in the staggering opportunity costs. It has also become an expectation of other nations. Our allies reasonably believe that they are entitled to rely on American blood and treasure, our will and weaponry. They set their own budgetary priorities accordingly—even when they are on or near the front lines of armed conflict.

In *Base Nation*, author David Vine summarizes one manifestation of the United States' far-reaching international commitments:

> [The] massive global deployment of military force was unknown in U.S. history before World War II. Now,

> seventy years after that war, there are still, according to the Pentagon, 174 U.S. bases in Germany, 113 in Japan, and 83 in South Korea. There are hundreds more dotting the planet in Aruba and Australia, Bahrain and Bulgaria, Colombia, Kenya, and Qatar, to name just a few. Worldwide, we have bases in more than seventy countries. Although few U.S. citizens realize it, we probably have more bases in other people's lands than any other people, nation, or empire in world history.

It may be that every dollar of these expenditures is entirely merited. Nonetheless, it's striking how few Americans comprehend the reach of our national power projection.

Despite the massive claim on national resources, there is little public debate on international strategy. Without strategy, it's difficult to set priorities. Without priorities, there is diminished accountability. Absent accountability, citizens cease to be sovereign.

Dwight Eisenhower served not only as supreme commander of Allied forces for Europe, but also as the first governor of the American Zone in Germany, the supreme Allied commander Europe for NATO, and the president of the United States. In 1953, following the death of Soviet premier Joseph Stalin, President Eisenhower reminded the world:

> Every gun that is made, every warship launched, every rocket fired, signifies in a final sense a theft from those who hunger and are not fed—those who are cold and not clothed. This world in arms is not spending its money alone—it is spending the sweat of its laborers, the genius of its scientists, the hopes of its children.

Referring to the costs attendant upon maintaining the British Empire at its apogee, Winston Churchill wrote a colleague in 1901: "For my own part, I see little glory in an Empire which can rule the waves and is unable to flush its own sewers."

Churchill's lament is timely for twenty-first-century America. It's chastening to juxtapose our often decrepit infrastructure with our gleaming ships and tanks and aircraft and missiles.

Difficult decisions loom. Will our policies be based upon publicly debated, well-considered strategic considerations? Or will we implicitly set priorities on the fly, as we respond to ever more remorseless budget pressures? Will we be hostage to events as all manner of special interests fight for resources amid declining government budgets?

To ask these questions is not to advocate one answer or another. It's to underscore the need for our people and our representative institutions to come together toward shared national purpose.

In his useful book *Superpower*, foreign policy analyst Ian Bremmer argues that the United States' predominant position requires fundamental choices informed by public debate. He proposes three alternative visions: "Independent America" (nation-building at home), "Moneyball America" (realist, relentless focus on national interest), and "Indispensable America (interventionist to advance American democratic values).

Such overdue reconsideration will occur in the context of changing notions of twenty-first-century leadership. In the twentieth century, "leadership" was conflated with dominance and dictation. Today, in the information age of decentralized information and institutions and power, leadership is also asserted through influence and example. We are, of course, familiar with these sea changes in America's innovative business and not-for-profit sectors. Yet our thinking about its implications for politics remains stagnant, especially in the most consequential area: our global leadership.

The time is certainly ripe for a comprehensive public discussion of these arrangements.

Our nation has been at war in the Middle East for more than a decade. There has been notably little congressional debate or oversight. Recent presidents, Republican and Democrat alike, have not offered a clear strategy that defines victory and affixes accountability. Many of our institutional and diplomatic arrangements are shopworn relics of the Cold War—even the Second World War.

Without dedicated taxes, our ongoing wars do not directly touch the lives of most Americans. There is little national sense of shared endeavor, much less sacrifice.

The number of veterans among elected and appointed public officials has declined from prior generations. Our circumstances bring to mind the injunction of the nineteenth-century British Army officer Sir William Francis Butler: "The nation that will insist on drawing a broad line of demarcation between the fighting man and the thinking man is liable to find its fighting done by fools and its thinking done by cowards."

Chinese strategist Sun Tzu observed, "There is no instance of a nation benefitting from prolonged warfare." There is no reason to suppose that America is exceptional in this respect.

As in other areas, our current circumstances are unsustainable. Polling confirms that the American people are skeptical of our current engagement in the world. Whether one broadly supports our approach or questions it, it's ripe for disciplined reconsideration—and, perhaps, a reset. Unlike some of the prior generations that have undertaken this task, we begin from a position of unprecedented economic, financial, military, and cultural strength, uniquely equipped to set our own course.

Social Mobility Strained

Benjamin Franklin observed that what matters in America is not who you are, but what you can do. Social mobility is part of our national makeup.

Today there is a widespread sense that this foundation of American life is giving way. Inequality is rising in respect of income and wealth. Stubborn unemployment and underemployment are seen by some as presaging long-term "secular stagnation." Of particular concern are the limited prospects of many Americans in their prime working years, from ages twenty-five to fifty-four.

Observers point to a range of causes. Some emphasize the distortions occasioned by a decade of artificially low interest rates imposed by the Federal Reserve. Others point to tax policies. Others look to the education system. Still others focus on rolling technological disruption amid an ever more global marketplace.

Whatever one's point of view, these issues merit comprehensive public debate. It has not been forthcoming from Washington. Democrats and Republicans alike decline to engage questions that could point toward policies that would be resisted by their special-interest sponsors.

Education System Underperforming

Education has always been the foundation of our nation's many achievements. At the moment, it's not performing at the high level necessary for rising generations to fulfill their promise.

American universities continue to lead the world in many categories. Inevitably, decades of success bring their own challenges. In particular, the economics of higher education are facing increasing scrutiny.

Many in the millennial generation have returned to live with their parents. This includes a large number who graduated college. They face uncertain prospects in troubled job markets.

As if that were not enough, many millennials are saddled with staggering debts to pay for higher education. The *Wall Street Journal* reports that the average level of student-loan debt exceeds $35,000. This is more than twice the amount of just two decades ago, adjusted for inflation. More than 70 percent of students carry such debt. The aggregate obligation of students and their parents has risen from less than $10 billion for the class of 1993 to more than $70 billion for the class of 2015. Such costs can be staggering for law graduates, for example. They may incur obligations over a hundred thousand dollars, with limited prospects of the high-paying employment many were led to expect.

Overall student debt now exceeds $1 trillion. The burden weighs heavily on rising generations who also face the prospect of unsustainable public debt. It has ripple effects on key life decisions. Many graduates are deferring marriage, children, and home ownership.

The rise in student debt has occurred in tandem with extraordinary inflation in the costs of higher education. They far exceed the benchmark consumer price index. There are numerous explanations. Some point to declines in state government funding. Others emphasize rising numbers of administrative personnel and salaries. Some discern a "bubble," created by the confluence of increased availability of loans with employer expectations of college degrees for entry-level positions.

These are systemic problems that require systemic responses. Washington, DC, has offered little more than tweaking the status quo. There has been little appetite for putting tough questions to those who benefit from a higher education system that reaches throughout our national life. Why have we not seen the presidents of our leading public and private universities hauled before congressional hearings? Why are their books not being opened, so that we and our elected representatives can make our voices heard in the expenditure of precious public and private resources?

If the challenges of higher education are chronic, those of K–12 are acute. Public concern crystallized with the landmark 1983 Reagan administration report, *A Nation at Risk.* The blue-ribbon panel concluded: "If an unfriendly foreign power had attempted to impose on America the mediocre educational performance that exists today, we might well have viewed it as an act of war."

Despite persistent political controversy in the interim, the situation remains grievous a generation later. In 2012, an independent task force, convened by the Council on Foreign Relations, underscored the relationship between K–12 education and national security:

> In international tests of literacy, math, and science, American students rank far below the world's leaders in Finland, South Korea, and Shanghai. They spend fewer years studying a more limited range of foreign languages than students in most other wealthy countries and just 1.4 percent of them study abroad, mostly in Europe. Significant majorities of young Americans are unable to identify strategically or politically important countries, such as Iraq or Afghanistan, on a map of the world; enrollment in civics and government classes is declining.

There is a shortage of young people qualified for critical sectors requiring specialized skills, ranging from technology to the foreign service. The Council report relates a troubling statistic: "75 percent of U.S. citizens between the ages of seventeen and twenty-four are not qualified to join the military because they are physically unfit, have criminal records, or have inadequate levels of education."

The Organization of Economic Coordination and Development (OECD) reviews comparative national educational performance. In 2012, the OECD found that the United States is near the top for per-pupil spending among the thirty-four countries evaluated. Despite this, American students are in the middle ranks for reading and in the lower half for math and science.

American per-student K–12 spending has risen approximately fourfold since 1960. No one could argue credibly that outcomes have improved comparably.

Health-Care System Dysfunction

The American health-care system has long been a tale of two worlds. In one, there is world-leading innovation. Patients with access to new drugs and devices may have their lives changed for the better.

At the same time, millions endure a troubled system. They may turn to emergency rooms for assistance that is better suited to other venues. They may be one illness away from financial ruin.

A comparative review from Bloomberg in 2012 ranked the US health-care system forty-fourth among fifty-one nations studied. Two years prior to the implementation of the Affordable Care Act ("Obamacare"), the United States spent nearly $9,000 per person per year for health care, with a life expectancy of 78.7 years. By contrast, top-ranking Singapore spent under $2,500 per person per year, with a life expectancy of 81.2 years.

Obamacare is, necessarily, a work in progress. Some aspects, such as the removal of outdated insurance exclusions for preexisting conditions, are unexceptionable. Others—such as the failure to meet public promises that individuals could elect to maintain their existing policies, and that their premiums would be reduced—remain nettlesome and unresolved.

Legal journalist Steven Brill poses a telling question: "Should we be embarrassed and maybe even enraged that the only way our country's leaders in Washington could reform healthcare was by making backroom deals with all the interests who wanted to make sure that reform didn't interfere with their profiteering?"

Ultimately, access to health care was expanded; wealth was redistributed. Yet the overall system is at least as convoluted and unaccountable as previously. Overarching challenges—such as the relatively high resources allocated to older people versus the young—remain unresolved. The plethora of providers—from the Veteran's Administration to Medicare and Medicaid to Obamacare to private alternatives—have not been rationalized. The intersection of the legal and health-care systems remains disordered.

How the health-care system will eventually be reformed remains unclear. A risk, as in other areas, is that decisions will be forced by budgetary exigencies and the rush of events, rather than thoughtful public policy debate focused on the future.

A Nation of Lawyers

I think that the species of oppression by which democratic nations are menaced is unlike anything that ever existed in the world…
The supreme power then extends its arm over the whole community. It covers the surface of society with a network of small, complicated rules, minute and uniform, through which the most original minds and the most energetic characters cannot penetrate to rise above the crowd. The will of man is not shattered, but softened, bent, and guided; men are seldom forced by it to act, but they are constantly

restrained from acting. Such a power does not destroy, but it prevents existence; it does not tyrannize, but it compresses, enervates, extinguishes, and stupefies a people, till each nation is reduced to be nothing better than a flock of timid and industrious animals, of which government is the shepherd.

—Alexis de Tocqueville

A number of the most prominent among our nation's founders were lawyers. They were indispensable to formulating the revolutionary theories and institutions in whose name an American nation would arise from the yoke of British rule.

Inevitably, as Tocqueville recognized, the legal profession emerged as a homegrown aristocracy in the new, constitutional order of things. As our political system evolved, lawyers played outsized roles. This is seen today in the routinely high numbers of lawyers in government, from presidents and vice presidents through the Congress and the agencies.

It used to be said that America had a government of laws, not of men. Today, it often seems we have a government of lawyers, not of law.

The American Constitution is structured on interlocking, countervailing powers. Looking to history as they forged the future, the founders sought to restrain the tendencies and temptations attending those temporarily entrusted with public authority.

The humility implicit in such arrangements is increasingly challenged by the practice of regulating more and more aspects of our lives through formal legal processes. In the trenchant observation of legal reformer Philip K. Howard, ever more extensive regulation constitutes central planning by another name.

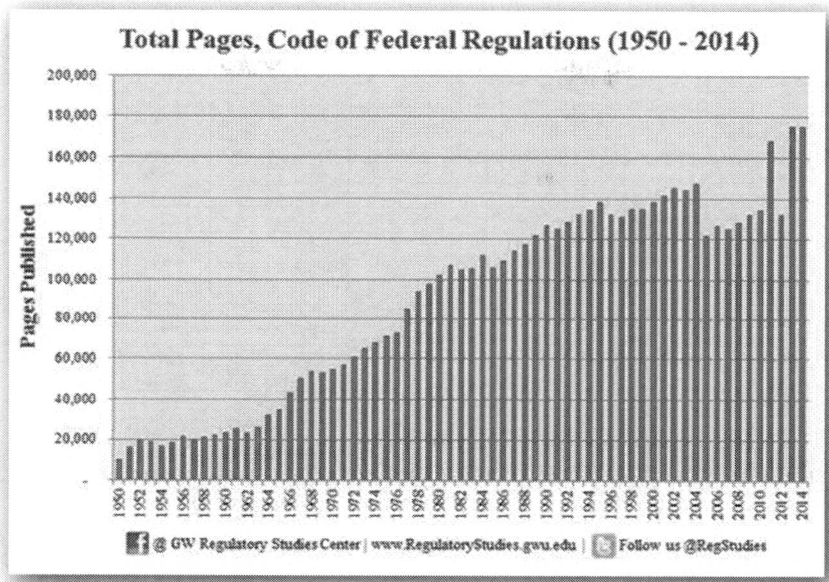

The expansion of the dominion of the law has occurred along with the increasing capacity of special interests to hijack governance for their own purposes.

The result is a great boon for the status quo. Established companies or industry sectors protect themselves through influencing the drafting, interpretation, implementation, and enforcement of laws and regulations. The metabolism of national life is slowed. Disruptive forces are entangled in legal and bureaucratic process.

This may be accomplished directly or through the imposition of requirements that appear, on their face, to have uniform effects. Either way, potential disruptors are penalized. As the technology industry has found, it becomes necessary for even the most productive "pirates" of change to enter the political arena to obtain access to consumers who can benefit from their products.

Unsettled areas of the law may create shadowy spaces where well-financed firms can shake down smaller businesses. For example, uncertainty in applying copyright, trademark, and patent laws and regulations can make good-faith compliance difficult if not impossible. Unscrupulous trolls lurk in the back alleys, inflicting trumped-up infringement claims. The result is yet more power and resources to the well-heeled, well-connected, and cunning who live off others' value creation.

In other areas, the law is clear, but rights are, practically speaking, unenforceable. The prohibitive cost of legal services means there may be no practical recourse against a large enterprise that abuses its power. If one is harmed by a public entity, there may be no legal recourse whatsoever. Given the rising reach of government power—often in alliance with powerful special interests—this is not a minor matter.

On the other side, financially successful individuals and enterprises may be habitually harassed by parasitic lawsuits prompted by their prominence. Some with an envious cast of mind might see this to as rough justice of sorts. The reality is that value creation is being penalized or stifled. In a time when global competition is a mouse click away, such misdirected effort imposes costs on all Americans.

As the infestation of lawyers and legalism remorselessly reaches further and further into our lives and work, the profession's historic ethic of disinterested service is declining. The lawyer-statesman ideal is in eclipse. In its place, we see the triumph of attorneys as advocates, disconnected from the morality of their arguments. Rather than relying on law as creating the outside boundaries for conduct, it is asserted as a substitute for high ethical standards. Legal norms intended for judicial settings are dubious when they are transported into other contexts.

The American legal system has long been a model for the world. Our institutions, including government agencies, have often been replicated by other nations. Increasingly, the American legal system is viewed as a cautionary tale. Competitive advantages we have become accustomed to—such as other nations adopting our regulations or regulatory decisions—are disappearing. Other nations are filling the void.

We're caught in a vicious cycle. People seek protection in the law—or refuge from the law. More and more and more laws pile up, one atop another. The legal system is intended to serve the public. Instead, we are all too often tied up in legal process—which, in turn, serves special interests of all kinds.

Jailer to the World

How did it come to pass that the nation symbolized by the Statue of Liberty has become the greatest jailer of the world?

According to the Institute for Criminal Policy Research, the United States incarcerates more than two million individuals. China is a distant second.

If our jails and prisons were incubators of rehabilitation, such numbers might be more defensible. Violence, including rape and gang activity, is rampant in many American correctional facilities. They are state-of-the-art training grounds for advanced criminality. Regrettably, as reported by the National Institute of Justice, recidivism is the norm. Individuals become ensnared in this destructive cycle, which can easily cross generations.

The waste of human talent is tragic. For many years, a standard talking point of politicians has been to compare the cost of maintaining criminals in prison with the cost of sending students to Harvard.

Rhetoric and reality collided in 2015. A group of maximum-security inmates in a New York prison defeated the Harvard debate team. The prisoners had previously bested West Point.

How much talent lies undiscovered and underutilized in these grotesque warehouses? How might it be recovered and redirected toward the communities that are torn apart—first by the violence of offenders, then by their absence as husbands and fathers and providers and mentors?

Immigration Chaos

Americans take justifiable pride in ours being a nation of immigrants. Our political system has squandered this great national advantage in a decades-long descent into disorder and division. There is no area where the separation between the politicians and the public is greater.

Facts about gray areas of the law are hard to establish with precision. What is clear is that would-be immigrants who are in the United States illegally constitute a massive population segment. The Pew Research Center reports that the number has "stabilized" in the past decade, at approximately 11.3 million in 2014.

Pew confirms that six states—California, Texas, Florida, New York, New Jersey, and Illinois—account for 60 percent of the unauthorized immigrant population. The distribution is expanding and changing over time. Individuals in this category constitute approximately 5 percent of the workforce. Approximately 7 percent of K–12 students have at least one parent in the nation illegally, with higher numbers in California, Texas, and Arizona.

Such a massive, longstanding presence inevitably causes distortions in law and public services. Undocumented individuals and families live and work in a twilight where law enforcement represents a threat. Having broken laws in the first instance, they cannot rely on authorities for protection against various forms of abuse.

In many communities, public services—from schools to hospitals—are stretched to the breaking point by the influx of noncitizens. Americans reliant on such vital services are affected the most. They may also face downward pressure on wages from low-cost competition in the marketplace. By contrast, the positive economic results from undocumented workers may be dispersed more broadly.

At the top of the socioeconomic ladder, the vibrant technology sector finds it difficult to obtain visas for highly educated talent. Foreign graduates of American universities may find it easier to earn advanced degrees in technical fields than to get a visa to put their skills to work in the United States.

Immigration policy is constitutionally reposed with the national government. Yet, many of the consequences are felt most keenly in distant states and communities. Presidents and congressional majorities of Democrats and Republicans have not achieved a comprehensive reform since President Reagan signed the Simpson-Mazzoli Act of 1986.

Conventional politics having failed, stakeholders turn to all manner of expedients to advance their interests. For example, advocates attempt to obtain rhetorical advantage. Some refer to "illegal aliens"; others to "illegal immigrants"; others to "undocumented immigrants"; still others to "unauthorized immigrants."

The *Los Angeles Times* reported in 2014 that the George W. Bush and Obama administrations redefined "deportations." Federal agencies had announced dramatically increasing numbers of individuals deported. Obama was characterized as "deporter-in-chief" by immigration rights advocates. In fact, the statistics were altered to include the "catch and release" of those detained and turned around at the border. The *Times* found, "Expulsions of people who are settled and working in the United States have fallen steadily since [Obama's] first term in office, and are down more than 40% since 2009."

Attempts to manipulate or limit the terms of public discussion reinforce the sense that those who make and enforce immigration laws are disconnected from those who experience their effects. Polls show high public support for stricter law enforcement of our borders. Polls also show high public support for regularizing the legal status of many illegal immigrants. A special-interest stalemate, played out through partisan politics, prevents accomplishment of either of these goals.

One of the tragic consequences of our broken immigration system is that it undercuts public confidence in the federal government's capacity to secure our borders generally. This prompts some Americans to turn against all immigration, legal or illegal. It also creates reasonable concern about the vetting process for all newcomers, including political refugees.

Nonetheless, the unsatisfactory status quo remains. Washington's dysfunction yields short-term benefit to a variety of special interests, notably including various industries and unions. The distress of citizens and undocumented residents alike remains unaddressed. Many of the costs of these unsustainable arrangements will fall upon rising generations.

Lack of Systems Thinking

The *Merriam-Webster Dictionary* defines "system" as "a regularly interacting or interdependent group of items forming a unified whole." To comprehend and respond effectively to large-scale, complex issues, government must employ systems thinking.

Our current politics and government are strikingly deficient in this regard. Each of the preceding challenges requires a systemic response. So, too, do many other public issues.

In recent decades, the Congress and the president, irrespective of partisan affiliation, have repeatedly proven ineffective in this respect. They tend to put forward policies that advance the short-term goals of their special-interest sponsors and allies. Deliberative processes are overridden in the legislative and executive branches. Congressional committees operate haphazardly. Members don't debate in any meaningful sense. Rather, they declaim on behalf of prefabricated policy positions, sometimes wrapped in philosophical niceties.

Presidents might be expected to impose systems thinking on major issues. They uniquely can expand and recast public understanding, using the "bully pulpit." In the early years of the twenty-first century, this has not occurred.

The absence of systems thinking has consequences. Accountability is limited. There is scant attention to data collection and analysis. Outputs are hazy. There is little public debate defining success. Silos arise within and between organizations. So-called mission creep ensues. Special interests arise and intensify in their reliance on access to public resources. Political debate tends to focus on the issues and perspectives presented by affected interest groups, rather than analyze programmatic performance.

Such problems are seen in the run-up to and execution of America's longest war, our ongoing engagement in the Middle East theater. So, too, it is with the "war on drugs," the "war on poverty," and the "war on cancer." The latter enterprises have been underway for as long as half a century, with no end in sight.

The passage and implementation of Obamacare is an apt example. It is intended to reform the entire health insurance system of the United States. As such, it encompasses a range of industries, from pharmaceuticals to medical device manufacturing, from insurance to food and beverage, as well as the legal and medical professions. There are, in fact, a series of simultaneously operating health-care systems, such as that of the Veterans Administration, Medicare, Medicaid, and for the active military and civilian employees and dependents. Obamacare, like other such initiatives in recent years, added complexity to and attenuated accountability within an already troubled and unaccountable situation.

Another current example can be found in the energy space. On the one hand, the national government is undertaking action to reduce the risks of climate disruption by limiting carbon dioxide emissions. In that pursuit, the current administration imposed new limits on oil drilling and pipelines. At the same time, another part of the same administration was working to lift economic sanctions on Iran. The latter policy will likely result is downward pressure on the market price for petroleum, thereby increasing carbon dioxide emissions. From the environmental perspective, the locations and sources of the emissions are irrelevant.

When public issues are defined by interest groups, focus may be diverted to one or a few aspects of a larger system. Perhaps it's not reasonable to expect advocates to look after the American commonwealth as a whole. Perhaps they truly believe that their self-interest is aligned with the public interest.

Yet, we should demand more from our government. It is tasked with reconciling the welter of factional demands within a broader conception of the national interest. It's not enough for our presidents and Congress to outsource housing policy to the National Association of Realtors. It's not enough to outsource entitlement policy to the AARP. Nor is it sufficient to bring in contending groups—such as the National Rifle Association and the Violence Policy Center—and set a policy within the bounds they establish.

On issue after issue, systems thinking is absent. Can we deal effectively with the poverty rate among children without factoring in entitlements for older people or the impact of legal and illegal immigration?

Can we dedicate more resources to children's health without a public exploration of the outsized resources dedicated to end-of-life care?

Our government is failing to apply systems thinking to the challenges of our time. Yet, in its durable dysfunction, our evolving governance is becoming a rogue system unto itself.

If a company were failing time and time and time again, one would anticipate that its revenues would fall. It would become threadbare and impoverished. Its headquarters might decline into a ghost town.

By contrast, our elected officials and their ecosystem of governance are thriving as never before.

Washington, DC

When the United States was established, the founders took care to separate the seat of government from the seat of finance. This example was followed by many states.

In recent years, Wall Street and Washington have merged. The Tea Party and Occupy Wall Street each comprehended aspects of this portentous change, even as their prescribed remedies diverged.

By many measures, dissatisfaction with our government in Washington has never been greater. Yet, almost in tandem, the Washington metro area has become distinguished for its combination of high income and conspicuous wealth.

The most recent listing from the Census Bureau, for 2012, documents the astonishing transformation underway. Five of the ten wealthiest counties in the nation are in the Washington metro area. Overall, the numbers rise to eleven of the top twenty-five counties.

The Sunlight Foundation examined the underlying economics:

> Between 2007 and 2012, 200 of America's most politically active corporations spent a combined total of $5.8 billion on federal lobbying and campaign contributions...[W]hat they gave pales compared to what those same corporations got: $4.4 trillion in federal business and support.

The investment was well-placed. According to the foundation, "for every dollar spent on influencing politics, the nation's most politically active corporations received $760 from the government."

Mark Leibowich, who brilliantly chronicles the new Gilded Age in Washington, wrote in the *New York Times* in 2014:

> There was a time, it's worth remembering, when outgoing public officials would return to their farms, stores, law firms, medical practices or whatever quaint things the founders envisioned our citizen leaders doing after their public lives ended...In 1974, according to the *Atlantic*, 3 percent of retiring members of Congress became lobbyists. Now half of all senators and 42 percent of representatives enter the field.

In his landmark book *The Rise and Decline of Nations*, Mancur Olson discerned the bigger picture:

> Lobbying increases the complexity of regulation and the scope of government...An increase in the payoffs from lobbying, as compared with the payoffs from production, means more resources are devoted to politics and cartel activity and fewer resources are devoted to production. This in turn influences the attitudes and culture that evolve in the society.

Polarization without Progress

Our country is afflicted by intense political polarization. If the division and rancor were a prelude to resolving great issues, they might be defensible.

Instead, we are enduring polarization without progress.

That is not to say it is polarization without purpose. In Washington, DC—for those who hold office, and the broader political class that has emerged—polarization can be profitable.

In the early twentieth century, writer, journalist, and reformer Upton Sinclair observed: "It is difficult to get a man to understand something, when his salary depends on his not understanding it."

In the early twenty-first century, Sinclair's lament is apt to an extent that he could not have conceived. Washington, DC deploys resources of the taxpayers to serve special interests. In turn, the special interests serve the political class. Together, they erect a citadel to defend the status quo. We the People are on the outside.

A tipping point may have been reached. Each of the three most recent presidents entered office with congressional majorities for their parties. For the first time in American history, the voters withdrew those majorities from three successive presidents.

No one can credibly say the voters aren't taking every opportunity before us to send distress signals.

The Great Reckoning

For a number of years, many of us have contemplated our governmental dysfunction, alternating between outrage and resignation.

Many rationalize inaction. Until we face a universally recognized crisis, they say, we cannot expect fundamental change. In the meantime, we make do. We turn more often to lower levels of government.

We look to the private sector to take on additional tasks. We benefit from the fact that, for all the faults of our governance, the United States remains a sought-after destination for talent and capital amid global instability.

Such fatalism is dangerous. It's the farthest thing from leadership. In unflattering contrast to our forebears, it means turning the fate of future generations to the kindness of bankers and lawyers and politicians and other strangers who are not motivated to serve the interests of the United States of America.

What is to be done?

There is at least one example of transformative leadership that was not imposed by a universally recognized crisis: Theodore Roosevelt's historic achievement, placing environmental protection and preservation on the national agenda.

Roosevelt was not elected to advance his conservation agenda. He was not responding to general public sentiment. He was not acting on behalf of special-interest sponsors. His vision and actions provoked foreseeable, intense political resistance that imperiled his larger agenda.

TR persevered. He robustly asserted the chief executive's inherent authority to safeguard and expand the inheritance of rising generations. He strove mightily to present his vision and earn citizen support. Taking the perspective of the future, he presented environmental stewardship as a moral issue. As such, it was a foundation on which other policies relied.

Let me say it so you won't have to: *We don't have a Theodore Roosevelt in our midst.*

What is more, the reforming, twenty-first-century leadership we have been waiting for will not come from Washington. It will not come from the top down. It will not come from the inside out.

The founders selected the first words of the Constitution with care: *We the People.* Ultimately, We the People are the authors and guarantors of our nation's ideals and institutions.

The far-sighted individuals who created the "Miracle at Philadelphia" in the summer of 1787 cast principles for the ages. Nevertheless, even their capacious imaginations could not have conceived the information age possibilities arrayed before us.

We have the opportunity—indeed, the obligation—to apply twenty-first-century leadership principles and tools to reset our government. Industry after industry has been disrupted in this way. We can treat those experiences as a prelude to the ultimate challenge: disrupting our politics and government.

Contrary to widespread opinion, this will not be accomplished by sending more "moderates" to represent us in Washington. Our challenge is far greater than merely cutting more deals with the powers that be.

To disrupt our failed governance, we need more independents. Independent of what?

Independent of the Special Interest State
that has displaced our constitutional operating system.

Disrupt Politics

The Great Reckoning

Theme

The decades-long failure of American governance has resulted in paralytic deadlock on a series of major national challenges. Special-interest groups collude with public officials to safeguard the status quo.

More and more of the costs and consequences of today's actions and inaction will fall to future generations. Reforming our politics and government is an indispensable first step to undertaking necessary changes in a range of policy areas.

Elements

- American government has turned to ever-rising debt to avoid hard decisions. This amounts to taxation without representation of future generations.
- Rotating political parties and politicians has not been effective in changing government. Our politics must be fixed in order for us make progress.
- Will we undertake reform in advance of a universally recognized crisis of historic magnitude? The information age equips us with more tools than ever before.
- Systems thinking is absent from our governance. Special interests frame issues in their own image.
- Our governance in Washington has become a system. It will not be repaired by an infusion of "moderates" who cut deals with the powers that be. Instead we need to empower leaders who are independent of the Special Interest State.

The Bosses of the Senate by Joseph Keppler, *Puck*, 1889

Two

The Special Interest State

In the history of mankind many republics have risen, have flourished for a less or greater time, and then have fallen because their citizens lost the power of governing themselves and thereby of governing their state; and in no way has this loss of power been so often and so clearly shown as in the tendency to turn the government into a government primarily for the benefit of one class instead of a government for the benefit of the people as a whole.

—Theodore Roosevelt

In politics, nothing happens by accident. If it happens, you can bet it was planned that way.

—Franklin D. Roosevelt

The 1944 Democratic National Convention in Chicago was destined to be historic.

President Franklin D. Roosevelt was seeking an unprecedented fourth term. FDR had seen the nation through the depths of the Great Depression. He took office in 1933, mere weeks after Adolf Hitler became chancellor of Germany. Now, in the summer of D-day, Roosevelt's long-sought victory over the Nazi gangster regime was in sight. The Fuhrer's "thousand-year Reich" lay in smoldering ruins. For Americans, close to home and around the world, there would be new worlds to create.

At this moment of national and personal triumph, a universal if largely unspoken question was in the air: Would Roosevelt survive another term?

One thing was clear: the choice of a vice presidential candidate for Roosevelt 4.0 might well be a fateful decision. Would the Democrats, in effect, be selecting two presidents?

As a result, the vice presidential nomination was vigorously contested. It was the great issue in suspense as the Democrats gathered in Chicago.

Missouri Senator Harry S Truman emerged as the consensus favorite of party bosses and elders. This occasioned a rare moment when FDR, the acknowledged virtuoso of American politics, let slip a telling comment.

The *New York Times* reported that Roosevelt instructed his aides to ensure that labor leader Sidney Hillman signed off on the vice presidential pick: "Clear it with Sidney."

Who was Sidney? Who was this individual with whom the most powerful leader in America—nay, the most powerful leader in the world—would consult in reaching such a momentous decision?

He was Sidney Hillman, the high-profile head of the Amalgamated Clothing Workers of America. Fiercely combative, ferociously committed to his causes, he routinely courted controversy.

"Good government" Republicans and conservatives were apoplectic. That the president of the United States would outsource his authority to a special-interest boss unleashed visceral outrage. That FDR would do so publicly suggested an insouciant arrogance.

The Republican presidential candidate, the crime-busting prosecutor turned politician Thomas E. Dewey, ensured that the story got the widest possible circulation. In the heat of partisan warfare, it was embellished: "Clear *everything* with Sidney."

From today's perspective, how quaint, how touchingly innocent is FDR's Sidney Hillman reference! Now, every politician "clears it with Sidney." There are a lot more Sidneys, in the sense that there are innumerable special-interest groups that are consulted at every stage, at every level of politics and government.

FDR's gaffe was an illuminating thunderbolt of inadvertent truth telling. He acknowledged what was becoming clear over the course of several decades: Special interests were increasingly dominating the nation's governance. That was troubling if not scandalous in the midst of the "good war" that elicited untold citizen sacrifice.

In our time, the undue influence of special interests is exerted through the Democratic and Republican parties alike. It is no longer capable of credible dismissal as an aberration; it is a system.

That system is the Special Interest State.

The System Is Broken—Long Live the System

It is a universally recognized fact: The American system of governance is broken.

Remember the simple diagrams of civics textbooks: how a bill becomes a law? Then, how a law is implemented, enforced, finally reviewed by courts? The inevitable conclusion was inspiring: Everyone's life is made better by the working of this glorious, constitutional machinery.

Such a rendering always tended toward sentimentality. Now it is farcical, a grotesque caricature.

In recent years the voters have experimented with all manner of partisan alignments to get things right. We've voted out the Republicans and voted in the Democrats—then back around again. We've had Democratic presidents with Democratic majorities in the two houses of Congress. We've had Republican presidents with Republican majorities in Congress. We've had split partisan rule of White House and Congress.

For more than a decade, all the partisan churning has not yielded accomplishments, much less progress. The constitutional system remains manifestly broken. Diehard partisans offer strained arguments that the fault lies with the other of the legacy parties. When their side fails, some say it simply can't be done.

At this point, it is difficult to grant credence to such tired partisan claims.

Recent presidents Barack Obama and George W. Bush are quite different in the minds and hearts of their core supporters. And yet, when one stands back a step, the similarities marking their administrations are unmistakable.

From rising debt levels to international and domestic security policies, there is far more continuity than change.

It is as if our politics has degenerated into a reality television show. The presidents are little more than front men—presenters standing atop the parasitic Special Interest State. They're pleasant but not compelling. They provide commentary and amusing asides on the passing scene. They often speak of the federal government and politics as if they're not participants, much less in charge.

At this point, we are conditioned by recent, recurring experience not to demand more.

The sentiment expressed by Jane Austen in another context is apt: *Washington, DC, has delighted us long enough.*

The Operating System of the Special Interest State

Disrupt Politics

One of the fundamental necessities in a representative government such as ours is to make certain that [those] to whom the people delegate their power shall serve the people by whom they are elected, and not the special interests.

—Theodore Roosevelt

Most of us understand that our official system is broken. This is surely a driving reason why a solid plurality of American voters self-identify as independents.

What may be less clear is the successor system—the Special Interest State—that has arisen in our midst. Just because it is not in the civics textbooks doesn't make it any less real.

The new system was not created by We the People. Nor have we been asked to ratify it. We're unable to hold it to account. We're reduced to being hapless bystanders—or, perhaps, unwilling subjects. The Special Interest State careens wildly about, obscured amid a fog of pious declarations of dedication to the greater good and our children.

It's difficult to comprehend the totality of what is now before us. Those who are pulling the strings aren't motivated to let us in on what they're up to.

Nonetheless, we've seen enough that we can begin to define the new operating system arising in our midst:

> The Special Interest State is a system of governance whereby the government yields its powers and prerogatives to special interests. Rather than serving as guardians of the general, public interest, government officials abdicate their fiduciary obligations. Indeed, government agencies themselves may not only be captured by special interests, but may also advance their own

> organizational agendas as special interests. The encroachment of special interests increases over time, as obstacles give way. They form electoral coalitions through the legal privileges and subsidies granted to support the Republican and Democratic parties within the so-called two-party system. Special-interest agendas are cloaked and implemented within partisan platforms.

The Special Interest State is operating as you read these lines. Never mind that it is not explicit. It is not located in an office building with its name on the door. It does not have a fixed address or a Delaware corporate registration. There's not a dedicated website. No one seeks credit, publicly claiming to be among its founders or stewards.

Its triumph has been gradual; now it is complete. Like the commonplace metaphor of water gradually heating until a numbed frog expires from boiling, the transformation has occurred over a lulling length of time.

If you seek a monument to the Special Interest State, behold Washington, DC. As the nation has come out from the deepest economic and financial crisis in a generation, the capital metropolis has emerged with heretofore unimagined wealth. The city of government, whose mission is to serve the nation, ever more resembles the seat of an aristocratic class.

Yes, our system of government is broken. It has been superseded by a new system. The new system is working well for those who guide and perpetuate it. Unfortunately, it is operating against the interests of the American people.

Who's a Special Interest?

There are numerous definitions of "special interest." They converge on one fundamental:

> Special interests are groups or empowered individuals who seek to direct government power to advance their own values. They seek to deploy the power of government to compel others to undertake actions or pay subsidies. Such special interests generally lobby government officials in pursuit of their goals. They may represent large groups or narrow segments of the population. In unusual cases, they may advocate on behalf of specific families and individuals.

In all cases, the term "special interest" carries a negative connotation. Its antithesis is the "general interest" or the "public interest." The term suggests that some will be advantaged over others. A special interest conduces to self-interest, to selfishness.

Many if not most people don't recognize themselves as part of special interests. Ask a teachers union member if he's a member of a special-interest group. He may well say, "Certainly not, I'm working for the children, for our shared future."

Ask an independent businessperson if her membership in the chamber of commerce makes her part of a special-interest group. She may well respond, "Certainly not, I'm working for the material well-being that all our goals for the next generation are built on."

Both the teacher and the entrepreneur would likely dismiss any comparison as "false equivalence."

Of course, they're *both* special interests. There is no one among us who's not represented by one special-interest group or another.

There's nothing inherently wrong with that. Special interests—and their ecosystem of lobbying—are a vital part of any government based on consent of the governed. Nazi Germany and the Soviet Union had no lobbyists or interest groups as we understand them. In each case, part of their initial appeal was their promise to sweep away corrupt, parasitic political classes.

The problem in American governance is not special interests per se. It is that our officials, in their pursuit of power and position, have yielded far too many of their responsibilities to a kaleidoscope of special interests.

Consider, for the moment, how Democrats and Republicans *quarrel* about trivialities. Yet they will not *fight* about the great issues of the day. In the regrettably apt parlance of the day, the politicians repeatedly "kick the can" down the road.

Compromise, more often than not, simply means placing costs and burdens on less powerful, less connected, less organized, more vulnerable groups. If there is not enough available from those remaining at the table, the politicians don't hesitate to shove the costs forward to future generations. To those groping through a dense fog of self-interest, the well-being of rising generations might seem hypothetical. Unfortunately, the various debt burdens being cast onto their backs are all too real.

Special-interest domination has disordered the proper relationship between government and the citizens it is established to serve. The presidency, the House, the Senate...Each of the legacy parties takes the reins; each overreaches in the thrall of its dominant interest groups; each is succeeded by the other after yet another electoral repudiation. This uninspiring roundelay has been the nation's plight for decades.

Poll after poll shows citizen disaffection from the process. The clamor and division of political campaigns intensifies...but little seems to change. It's a closed-loop system beyond the reach of voters.

The Special Interest State has its own logic. It has its own goals. By its own terms, it's succeeding brilliantly.

The Special Interest State, having become a system unto itself, has spawned a political class. This ecosystem is based in Washington, DC, but its bloodstream courses through our national life. Digital-age tools constitute a carrier, giving it unprecedented reach.

The political class that has emerged around it has itself become a special interest of great magnitude and influence. Unlike the traditional professions, the political class has no enforceable obligation to serve the greater good. As a result, they are at least as committed to preserving the Special Interest State as they are to advancing the cause of any one interest group. Many lobbying organizations serve interests connected with both of the legacy parties.

At a moment of profound, historic change, at home and abroad, the Special Interest State is protecting an unsustainable status quo. This might not matter in quiet times, but it's an existential challenge for the global hyper power at the dawn of the twenty-first century.

But wait: *You ain't seen nothing yet.* The encroachment of government institutions into every aspect of American life is, subtly and inexorably, moving all of us into the suffocating embrace of the Special Interest State. With our awareness shaped by television and Internet controversies created and communicated by special interests, each of us looks to protect our own interests. The sense of shared national interest is being lost.

Will the Special Interest State remake America in its own image? Will we retreat to defend our own interests, abdicating the pursuit of the greater public interest? Or will We the People recover our power?

Will we transform Washington in America's image?

Who Is Washington Serving?

American government is founded on the notion of the consent of the governed. We the People grant our prerogatives to our government. The government is nothing more than an instrumentality to serve us. Our public servants add value by organizing and scaling our individual efforts in service of the national good.

Does that sound like Washington, DC, today?

The Special Interest State has upended historic notions of American governance. In theory, elections enable the American citizenry to reorient Washington, DC, as it strives to serve the nation. The culture in Washington should reflect a service orientation toward the values and aspirations of the American people.

The electoral process has been hijacked by special interests to such an extent that the power flow is reversing. Special interests select political candidates. In many cases, they help craft the contours of their legislative districts. Special interests also attain undue influence over government agencies, even encroaching on law enforcement.

It is a chastening but revealing exercise: as you analyze words and deeds emanating from Washington, pause to consider: *Who are they serving?*

The Corruption of the Legacy Parties

Citizens are right to observe that voting in one party or the other does not have the transformative effects promised in the heat of campaigns. There is ample reason for frustration with the performance of the legacy parties.

Mindless, self-serving partisanship is universally decried. Is it the fundamental problem? Or is it a symptom of the actual malady?

The two great political parties of American history are legacy enterprises, carrying forward the vision and customs of earlier times. They are shells through which special interests operate.

Gallup polls confirm what so many of us observe—or, at the least, intuit. Citizens are streaming out of the legacy parties. Among millennials—new voters evaluating the landscape with fresh eyes—the independent numbers are highest.

The dominance of governance by the legacy parties is based on an extensive, embedded wireframe of legal privileges and subsidies. It is reliant on the inertia imparted by public acquiescence in the so-called "two-party system." There is a widespread misperception that the organization of elected and appointed officials as Democrats and Republicans is based in the Constitution.

The legacy-party duopoly is nothing more than a cartel arrangement. It's sustained by government power—power wielded by officials who are themselves products of the party system. Such a scheme, examined objectively, is flagrantly inconsistent with American civic ideals. We would never choose such an arrangement if it were offered for our consideration ab initio.

For the time being, the legacy parties operate as the organizing entities in the Congress, the White House, and the states. They have buildings and websites and stationery. Politicians seek office under their banners.

The legacy parties constitute the ultimate closed shop. The rising numbers of independents are compelled to pay significant costs for legacy-party primaries and related election operations. It's hard to imagine a more outrageous violation of First Amendment expectations. Church and state are understood as separated, but party and state are accepted as united.

The false-front frippery and distracting hocus-pocus of the legacy parties bring to mind the fragile fraudulence of the Wizard of Oz.

Despite their durability as legal and organizing entities, the Republican Party and the Democratic Party no longer exist as such. Historically, they served as instruments of governance. Each of the legacy parties comprised a diversity of interests and opinions. They were mediating forces between the citizens and our government.

Today, the legacy parties have shrunken into cat's-paws for the special-interest groups that constitute their campaign coalitions. They are instrumentalities of the Special Interest State, separate from the public they ostensibly serve.

The interest groups conjoined within each party may initially have been linked by philosophy or accidents of history or by mass movements or the leadership of charismatic individuals. Over time, though, they remain allies out of unexamined habit and the permanent pursuit of power. The absence of meaningful competition has foreseeably fostered brittle inflexibility. The parties, like the special interests they serve, are more and more removed from the citizens they claim to represent. They attempt to control the public discussion, to manufacture consent.

Year after year, the Democratic and Republican parties line up like armies of old. Their interest groups unleash their familiar, tired rhetorical assaults in a stalemated, unending electoral war. The only times the parties reliably come together is when there's a threat to their shared privileges.

Ideally, political parties would continually evolve, competing to ensure that government is innovative and accountable. Instead, their privileged status has rendered them reactionary. Ever-sharper polarization is their preferred "new normal."

The activist base of the Republican Party seeks to restore a mythic version of 1950s-era social life in America—without racism. They resist innovation and change. They seek to use the power of government to impose their views by force of law, rather than undertake the more challenging tasks of moral suasion.

The activist base of the Democratic Party seeks to restore a mythic version of 1950s-era economics—without reducing today's much greater national wealth. They resist innovation and change. They seek to use the power of government to impose their views by force of law, rather than undertake the more challenging tasks of moral suasion.

To be sure, legacy-party activists don't see themselves this way. If anything, they may be enjoying an Indian summer of sorts. As the parties lose adherents, those who remain share worldviews that are intensely experienced and expressed.

This distillation makes its way into practical politics. For example, computers have combined with the evolution of voting rights laws to apply gerrymandering with scientific precision. In addition, many localities are trending toward one political affiliation or another, as like-minded, highly mobile Americans aggregate. Congressional districts tend to be drawn opportunistically. They may gather together or disperse citizens in districts that advance the goals of politicians, rather than the values shared within geographic, ethnic, or religious communities. Party politicians and their special-interest sponsors collude to craft districts in their own image.

Their preferred districts—now the vast majority in the US House of Representatives—are dominated by voters of one party. As a result, the elections that matter most are often the party primaries. The base of the locally dominant party can be the determining factor. Politicians and interest groups train a laser focus on their relationships and standing with these readily mobilized voters.

As advocacy enterprises for special interests, the legacy parties are enemies to institutional innovation and accountability. They don't answer, in a meaningful way, to citizens generally. Otherwise, polarization without competition would not be their stock-in-trade.

Does this strike you as hyperbolic? Try this test: go to a legacy-party headquarters and offer your interesting, heartfelt ideas on governance. You'll likely get the practiced, polite nodding of politicians and aides who have no concern with your thoughts. If, instead, you offer money—or represent an influential interest group—you'll gain their rapt attention.

Yes, Democrats and Republicans reliably, robotically wave American flags at their ritualized public gatherings. They speak in our name. They piously proclaim their faith in the future.

In fact, these hollowed-out husks merely provide cover for the real powers behind the curtain: special-interest groups.

It is through the legacy parties that special interests form alliances, set the national agenda, and operate the levers of government.

That is the essence of the operating system of the Special Interest State.

The Congress in the Special Interest State

Have you, dear reader, seriously considered a run for the Congress?

First things first: you would need to attend to money. If you are running for a seat in the House of Representatives, you'll need a way to reach out to targeted voters within an aggregation of more than seven hundred thousand people. This does not come cheap.

Raising money from individuals in small increments is immensely time consuming. Some would characterize it as soul destroying.

Well-intended reforms limit individual campaign donations to a few thousand dollars. That is just low enough to keep you on the phone for hours per day. Many politicians plan to dedicate as much as 70–90 percent of their time to fundraising during campaign season (and, more and more, it's *always* campaign season). The contribution limits are just high enough to force your attention to the relatively small number of people who can contemplate such expenditures.

You will soon find that there are special-interest groups ready to assist you.

They are solicitous Sherpas on the well-worn path to the gates of the Special Interest State. They can get the word out to their members and supporters. They can lend their imprimatur.

Their kindness comes at a price.

They will likely ask that you do far more than share a general philosophical approach to representative government. They will engage you, with incongruous politesse, in the uninspiring rites of passage of the Special Interest State.

You will be directed to fill out detailed questionnaires about your voting intentions, should you be elected. The special interests know, far more than you, what issues are likely to arise in the coming years. Little will be left to chance. Your signature closes the deal. Digital technology preserves your commitment for the duration of your career.

If you are intent on running, you will overcome your initial queasiness soon enough.

The interest groups can mobilize allies. For Republicans, that might be chambers of commerce and gun-rights groups and social conservative organizations. For Democrats, that might be unions and trial lawyers and environmental organizations. Candidates of both parties might look to the financial sector or dominant local industries.

In a myriad of small ways, the warm, welcoming embrace of interest groups can make your life as a candidate palpably easier. They can supply prefabricated information about the issues of the day. They can tell you what language persuades your target voters. Almost without noticing, you are soon reaching your constituents with words that work. Perhaps they've heard them before. They might have come to them on television, most likely via partisan organs such as MSNBC or Fox News. Or they might recognize them from their memberships in local and national organizations.

To determine the language with which candidates describe issues is power. It may have even greater influence than deciding future votes through enforcement of commitments on candidate questionnaires.

To set the boundaries of discussion is to delimit the notions that are entertained in public debate. In time, they can circumscribe the thoughts and imaginations of candidates and citizens.

Your alliances with special interests can add tremendous value to your campaign by putting boots on the ground. The so-called air game of television and radio must be supplemented with platoons of mobilized individuals who undertake the hard slog of retail politics, door to door, person to person, meeting to meeting. Today this includes sophisticated targeting and Internet communications.

Most congressional districts are not competitive in general elections. One or the other of the legacy parties holds structural advantages imposed through the states' legislative redistricting processes. Outsized resources can then be poured into the subset of competitive campaigns. Low-turnout party primaries might not look good in civics classes, but they're an essential building block of the Special Interest State.

Sometimes the special interests conceal their giving hand. Many turn to putatively independent issue advocacy organizations. Their resources may be deployed in a bombardment of television advertisements, for example. To be sure, such efforts are ostensibly barred from direct coordination with candidates. And yet, only the willfully blind cannot see what's going on. The situation is made all the worse because of an oddity in the evolution of the federal campaign finance laws: Contributions to some outside organizations can be unlimited and undisclosed; contributions to candidates' campaigns are limited and disclosed.

As a candidate, you may well regard these outside interventions as a mixed blessing. You welcome the resources. Perhaps you are relieved that such outside groups may take on the dirty work of tearing down your opponents.

You've got a reputation to uphold, a life to return to. By contrast, the special-interest groups, often operating from afar, have no such compunctions. Their political search-and-destroy missions are comparable to the use of drones to conduct targeted assassinations, with limited human contact. If you are skittish at first, there's nothing like being on the receiving end of a slanderous television ad to persuade you that the interest groups supporting your opponents are evil.

As a candidate, you might well find the lack of coordination with independent committees to be vexatious. Such groups may guide public concern toward issues that would not be your priority. They may express your positions in ways that limit your capacity for compromise, should you be elected. They may attack your opponent in ways you're uneasy with—and might well prompt or reinforce negative ads against you.

To navigate this minefield, you might hire consultants or campaign managers who are street smart in the shadowy byways of outside influence. For example, you might engage individuals who have run independent expenditure campaigns, who understand the code of unacknowledged coordination. Perhaps they've worked with "dark money." That is the money whose donors remain anonymous.

Who prevails in this process?

The victors are not solons rising from the mists of Periclean Athens into the marble halls of the Capitol in Washington. They tend to include individuals noted for the capacity to raise money effectively. Our elected officials are acculturated to maneuver among and on behalf of their interest-group overlords.

There may be some people whose desire to "serve" in Congress is such that this is not problematic. Perhaps their views on the issues are utterly conventional and suggestible, tightly in sync with talk radio and cable television hosts, spoon-fed by special interests. My informed hunch is that there are many others who are queasy. All too often, by the time they recognize the snares, candidates are swept up in the process.

Remember the iconic political movie *The Candidate*? It was mildly transgressive in its moment, amid the widespread—and well-founded—cynicism that took hold in the 1960s and 1970s.

On election night, challenger Bill McKay (Robert Redford) prevails, winning a US Senate seat.

As the film concludes, Senator-elect McKay faces a press conference. As he has through the campaign, he turns to his political consultant for direction: "Marvin…what do we do now?"

Today, the victorious candidate would not need to ask what she would do next.

In the Special Interest State, her path is preordained.

Welcome to Congress

Newly elected members will find their interest-group sponsors prepared to remain at their side during their transition into office.

Amid the fog of political warfare, did your campaign incur debts? Your interest-group allies may well help you through this gnawing inconvenience.

Perhaps you can benefit from training for new officials in the ways of Washington. Key interest groups are there to help. Various associations will bring you into reassuring contact with your party colleagues, who will have survived similar electoral combat experiences. Think tanks are prepared to lend a hand. Nominally nonpartisan, they are often financed by interest groups and associated donors who are allied within one or the other of the legacy parties.

Who will staff your new office? Perhaps some of your campaign team long to serve in Washington or in your district office. Perhaps you will look to career staff who have served other members. Old hands likely know the ins and outs of dealing with special interests. Such relationships tend to outlast the careers of passing politicians.

Perhaps you will follow the lead of those members who dispense with appearances, hiring staff directly from special-interest groups. This may compensate for the ongoing departure of other congressional staffers to the lucrative world of K Street lobbying.

To what committees will you be assigned? A choreographed dance ensues. Your obeisance to interest groups will be a decisive factor. So, too, your presumed fealty to your party leadership in the Congress will be evaluated. These two strands combine, inexorably restricting your freedom of maneuver.

Your days and nights will be filled beyond your prior experience. Hearings for various committees will be must-attend events. Everyone knows that a poor attendance record can be fodder for a future electoral opponent. It matters not at all that many of the hearings are pointless, staged events.

Nonetheless, you are dedicated to effectively questioning witnesses. You will be particularly attuned to your duties to oversee the executive branch. Your personal staff will be supplemented with committee staff who provide you with research and writing. They will work with interest groups on your behalf. They will frame issues with information from sympathetic sources. Their relationships with individual lobbyists—including former staff and members—are invaluable.

Your participation at hearings will be scrutinized by many stakeholders. Interest groups will be on the lookout for new stars. So, too, they will watch for deviations from orthodoxy. Their mind-set may be expressed directly or transmitted through the enforced party line. Partisan television and radio personalities—supplemented by social media ecosystems—will monitor your progress. Feedback will be freely provided.

Nowhere will that feedback arrive more directly than via your fundraising efforts. Given the high costs of television advertising—and the immense sums that can be targeted in the subset of competitive primaries or general elections—the result is a ceaseless treadmill.

Fundraising for breakfast. Fundraising for lunch. Fundraising receptions. Fundraising dinners. Fundraising outings with colleagues and lobbyists.

If you're in a safe seat, your party leaders will ask you to contribute to the campaign coffers of less fortunate colleagues. Or, perhaps, they will demand that you tithe into funds they personally control.

Your committee assignments will likely be linked to expectations for fundraising for the party. If you're on a major committee such as Ways and Means, those expectations can be high indeed. If you're in "leadership"—such as chair or ranking member (top minority-party slot), your fundraising from relevant interests must rise accordingly.

Needless to say, the "leaders" that emerge from this process owe their power to the special interests they are theoretically intended to govern. The result: Higher position and greater authority are achieved only through conspicuous deference to donors. A chairman of the House Financial Services Committee expressed his understanding of his role in the Special Interest State: "In Washington, the view is that the banks are to be regulated, and my view is that Washington and the regulators are there to serve to the banks."

There's more, of course. You are the advocate and protector of your constituents. Ill served by byzantine federal bureaucracies, they turn to you to get through the phone hell of the IRS, the broken websites of federal health insurance, the failed veteran's care providers. Others may simply want a tour of the Capitol or the White House.

Even these constituent services pull you back into the bosom of the Special Interest State. You're likely getting the most requests from wealthier folks or those otherwise connected to campaign resources. They are the most likely to have ties with the interest groups that have invested in your political project.

Is this the legislative career that motivated you to enter the arena? If you are idealistic, you may have envisioned yourself working late into the evening, furrowing your brow on matters of grave importance. The shades of Adams and Webster and Sumner would inspire you forward. You'd be drafting new laws to right the wrongs that your predecessors ignored or failed to rectify. More modestly, you might have seen yourself as an honest broker, challenging the torpid, self-reverential gridlock of Washington.

The bracing reality is, you're not likely to spend time reflecting on the *Federalist Papers.*

You're not likely to be conceiving ideas for legislation. Interest groups—directly or through affiliated think tanks or associations—will suggest topics for bills for you to "sponsor."

Nor will you be asked to trouble yourself with the tedious chore of drafting legislation. Even in your areas of expertise, statutory language will tend to be complex if not altogether incomprehensible.

You will come to rely on lobbyists and staff to sort it all out. Truth be told, you won't even read most of the legislation you sponsor, much less the mass of legislation you'll vote on. You are least likely to peruse the most important bills—health-care reform, energy policy, appropriations. Statutes in these areas tend to be too long, too convoluted to yield to common understanding. They are dense, clotted with arcane provisions, pockmarked with scores of special-interest tweaks.

All in all, it's not a pretty picture.

If you're like a rising number of representatives and senators, you might well wonder whether it makes more sense to move into lobbying. The pay is much better. You might well have more direct effect on the legislative process. And you could have a much easier life...

That kind of thinking inclines one to a subtle transition. You find yourself ever more appreciative of the folks in Washington who understand your life, your work, your sacrifices. You may come to relate as much to them as to your constituents back home. Since the interest groups can be decisive in your evolving relationship with your electorate, retreating ever further into their embrace may happen without your noticing...

This has become commonplace. A snapshot of our time: even highly ranked members of Congress from safe seats may choose to cash out, moving from Pennsylvania Avenue to K Street. Henceforth they can directly, openly advocate on behalf of the special interests they favored while serving in the name of the public.

Special-Interest Subjugation of the Congress

Who in Congress serves you, dear reader?

If you're tightly aligned with a particular interest group, you may feel well represented. Your congressman or senator may relentlessly advocate the policies with which you are most concerned. You can keep tabs on the Internet if you like, ensuring adherence to the supplied script.

The problem is, the Special Interest State has made such fealty the norm. That a single representative or senator is beholden to special-interest groups is troubling. That the entire Congress is in the thrall of special interests is a tragedy.

Among the consequences of special-interest subjugation of the Congress:

The legacy parties are monolithic. In the Special Interest State, elected officials are aligned with coalitions of interest groups. Each of the legacy parties has its required alliances. The special-interest domination of the Democrats and Republicans has resulted in lockstep conformity.

Even representatives from the relatively few, more competitive districts are brought into line. To be sure, their legislative overlords may allow some apparent deviations. Upon close examination, they invariably turn out to be inconsequential, intended to present a misleading sense of independence to swing voters. Thus, votes that are not required to pass controversial legislation may be exempted from the party discipline.

So, too, purely symbolic votes may be granted. For example, a handful of members may be allowed to vote against their party's chosen candidate for speaker—if the speaker's election is not in doubt.

There is scant diversity of point of view among senators and members of the House in either of the legacy parties. To be sure, the party that is out of power may look somewhat more flexible—but beware. Their stakes are lower. Out of power, pursuing power, their grandees may well countenance an appearance of diversity of thought. Back in charge, they are liable to rein things in.

It takes very little to be termed a "maverick" in such circumstances. Slight deviations will be called out. "Conservative" Democrats and "liberal" Republicans in Congress are all but extinct.

Debate is defunct. In theory, representative democracy should include wide-ranging, vigorous debate. Innovation would emerge from the contest of ideas.

Does that sound like today's Congress?

Congressional debate is a dead letter. The notion of a true give-and-take of ideas, forging creative approaches to public questions, has no place. To be sure, the forms remain. The substance has long since drained away. To the extent participants take their colleagues' views into account, it's simply to conjure up their responses. When members speak on the floor, covered by C-SPAN, they address their remarks to the television audience, not to one another.

Members tend to regurgitate talking points drafted by interest groups. Perhaps the presentations will be laundered, coming to the congressman's desk via the political parties and think tanks with whom the interests are aligned. Congressional hearings and related "fact-finding" are occasions for presenting interest group demands.

Legislation is corrupted. In 2012, the *Economist* sought to place the Dodd-Frank financial reform legislation in perspective:

> The law that set up America's banking system in 1864 ran to 29 pages; the Federal Reserve Act of 1913 went to 32 pages; the Banking Act that transformed American finance after the Wall Street Crash, commonly known as the Glass-Steagall Act, spread out to 37 pages. Dodd-Frank is 848 pages long. Voracious Chinese officials, who pay close attention to regulatory developments elsewhere, have remarked that the mammoth law, let alone its appended rules, seems to have been fully read by no one outside Beijing.

Glass-Steagall was summarized as follows: "An Act to provide for the safer and more effective use of the assets of banks, to regulate interbank control, to prevent the undue diversion of funds into speculative operations." This law served as the foundation of Wall Street regulation from 1933 through the end of the twentieth century.

The relative brevity and simplicity of Glass-Steagall should not be dismissed presumptuously as a relic of "a simpler time."

The Great Depression that followed the crash of 1929 constituted an existential challenge to America's financial system, our economic system, and our notions of representative government. It is generally accepted that the dismemberment of Glass-Steagall in the 1990s set the stage for much of the financial turbulence of the early twenty-first century.

By contrast, the extraordinary length and incomprehensible complexity of Dodd-Frank is emblematic of the Special Interest State.

One can be certain that every paragraph, every line, every comma and period and semicolon, was inserted in service of one or more special interests. Statutory and regulatory drafting has been monetized in the Special Interest State.

If each part has meaning, the law as a whole may not operate as an effective system. Or, more to the point, it may not operate as a system that is recognizable as such. There is no delineation of outputs from legislation. The "outputs" of the legislative process, from the point of view of the special interests, are merely inputs into laws. The result is a breakdown of public accountability.

In the Special Interest State, there is less financial corruption of individual members than at earlier times in our history. The congressmen who take cash in briefcases, who hide money in refrigerators, who die with money in shoeboxes…these are outliers.

Instead, the legislative process itself is corrupt, in the original sense of the word. It is broken, unable to function as intended. An institution established to serve the wider public interest is, increasingly, a place where members and lobbyists brazenly serve their own interests.

A recent Speaker of the House, discussing the enactment of Obamacare, inadvertently distilled the corruption that debilitates American representative democracy: "We have to pass the bill so that you can find out what's in it, away from the fog of controversy."

Roll over, Mr. Madison.

Oversight is ineffectual. In our constitutional framework, the legislative branch is the source of laws, and the president is entrusted with executing the laws. Congressional oversight of the executive is a fundamental, protective counterweight.

Increasingly, oversight has become ineffectual.

Legislative majorities are increasingly reluctant to hold presidents of the same party to account. During the Second World War, Democratic senators led the questioning of the policies of a Democratic president. Indeed, one of the most demanding overseers of the Roosevelt administration's conduct of the war, Senator Harry Truman, subsequently emerged as FDR's vice president. Such institutional and individual integrity is scarce today.

More common is "oversight" of the executive branch on behalf of aggrieved special interests. In some cases, this might mean advocating a particular interpretation of a statute. There is little accountability or comprehension of major laws, taken as a whole. Yet there can be energetic oversight of specific provisions that affect motivated interest groups.

Such special-interest advocacy has moved inexorably into areas formerly separated from politics. Increasingly it includes congressional interference with law enforcement. The historic wall between law enforcement and politics has been breached. Rather than publicly debate and reform civil and criminal provisions, members of Congress interpose themselves in the murky area of "enforcement discretion."

Those who are less attuned to niceties seek to control executive-branch enforcement in the dark alleys of the budget and appropriations process.

It is not an exaggeration to note that congressional oversight is not undertaken on behalf of the American people as a whole. Having served special interests in the drafting of laws, our public officials continue their service in implementation and enforcement.

Abandonment of constitutional prerogatives. As Congress does the bidding of special interests, it neglects its unique constitutional obligations. For example, its budget-making procedures are disordered.

Even more significantly, the Congress has, over the course of more than a half century, abandoned its war-powers responsibilities. The last time the United States enacted a declaration of war was in 1942.

The failure to follow constitutional requirements for declaring war might be less problematic were it accompanied by rigorous congressional oversight. Instead, such oversight has been long been lacking.

At this point, Congress is so far removed from effective participation in foreign affairs that it lacks members of recognized stature to credibly assume the role.

As a result, Congress routinely accedes to institutional retreat, the better to protect the reelection prospects of individual members. War-making powers are heedlessly yielded through elastic authorizations to presidents. Budget authority is surrendered via expedients such as "continuing resolutions" and "sequesters." Rather than confront knots of intense interest groups, the Congress even transferred its authority for base closures to nonelected ad hoc commissions.

In recovering its constitutional prerogatives, there is no better place to start than war powers. A good rule of thumb would be that Americans should not be asked to die in any conflict that has not been debated and defined through a declaration of war. As the founders intended, no lone individual, with all their flaws and limitations, should have the power to offer up American lives and treasure to the dogs of war.

The President in the Special Interest State

Domesticating Presidents

There used to be a position that was entrusted with bringing Congress and special interests into line with the national interest. It's called the presidency.

In this vital sense, it's been vacant for more than a decade.

It was not always this way. There was a time when presidents were viewed as bulwarks against the encroachment of special interests. Their relative independence was a safety valve against the failings of Congress. In the words of Harry Truman: "The President is the representative of the whole nation and he's the only lobbyist that all the 160 million people in this country have."

In the early twenty-first century, the presidency, too, has been incorporated into the Special Interest State. Perhaps it was inevitable. In a government of shared powers, if one branch is corrupted, it may be simply a matter of time before the others give way.

Consider the recent presidents, George W. Bush and Barack Obama. They are not presidential leaders in the sense we have sought in our history. They do not possess the gravitas we associate with consequential chief executives such as Franklin Roosevelt and Ronald Reagan.

By contrast, contemporary presidents are light popular entertainers. They provide running commentary on public affairs. They do not credibly direct the machinery of government.

Bush and Obama bear an uncanny resemblance to television talk show hosts. Perhaps Pat Sajak, the relentlessly anodyne presenter of *Wheel of Fortune*, is an appropriate point of comparison. Or you may think of Jack Barry, the disgraced host of *Quiz Show* fame.

To paraphrase Frank Zappa, presidential politics has become the entertainment division of the Special Interest State.

Is this an exaggeration? No.

The abdication of leadership by the presidents is just the beginning of the inquiry. The question becomes, who has moved into the power vacuum?

The answer, yet again, is that special interests are attaining increasing control over the levers of governance. This includes the executive-branch departments and the so-called independent agencies.

Ponder an overarching question: In confronting major issues, how often did George W. Bush and Barack Obama act counter to the special-interest coalitions to whom they owed their elections?

You will need the fingers on one hand, at most.

How the System Gets Its Man (or Woman)

Perhaps it is mere happenstance that our presidents are increasingly creatures of the Special Interest State.

On the other hand, Franklin Roosevelt's dictum may apply: "In politics, nothing happens by accident. If it happens, you can bet it was planned that way."

Consider how we come to regard individuals as "credible" contenders for the presidency. To reach a position of such vast responsibility and reach, there is no single, necessary path. No one, not even an effective past president, can have proven herself across the range of tasks awaiting a new commander in chief in an ever-changing world.

First, we look for relevant "experience." Some may regard congressional service as central. Others may look to those who've served as governors. Still others may place value on experience in business or the military.

It is no accident that Bush and Obama each began their political careers with races for the US House. That each was initially defeated is of little consequence. What matters is they were acculturated, from the start, to serve special interests. They accepted, thrived, and prevailed in the system in which they filled out extended forms, offering their fealty. They would pledge their future votes to special interests in order to obtain the support necessary to make their case to the wider electorate.

Bush and Obama took timeworn paths to the White House: through the state house and Capitol Hill. For all their differences in temperament and experience, each possesses dexterity in brokering deals among interest groups.

Having obtained the threshold experience deemed relevant by conventional opinion, presidential candidates enter the "money primary." They are not accorded status as "serious" because they have thought widely and wisely about our national future. They are evaluated for their capacity to raise massive amounts of campaign cash. Doing so enables them to make their case through television and voter mobilization. They can attract the best staff and consultants. They will garner early endorsements. Their promise and prominence may deter challengers.

How does one become positioned to prevail in the money primary?

The money flows from special interests. Longstanding relationships nurture mutual confidence.

Loyalty has its rewards.

Past Performance is the Best Indicator of Future Fealty

The day has long passed when candidates "stood" for president. Now they must "run." They are not sought out; they seek the office.

In theory, a presidential campaign is an educational process. The candidates propose ideas. The public reacts. The competition of candidacies serves the public interest. Ideally, the aspirants grow through the experience. Their character is hardened in the crucible of political combat.

In fact, special interests infest every nook and cranny of the process. The candidates who run the gauntlet cultivate the capacity to express opinions that are safely within the boundaries imposed by their sponsoring interests. They strive to convey authenticity while lip-syncing the words of others. The most skilled appear to maintain a semblance of independent judgment.

No one should underestimate how draining such a process can be on the candidates. The discipline demanded is grueling. Nearly every moment of their existence is tracked by video cameras supplying footage to their opponents. Just a moment off script can be used to depict them in the most negative light. If the error appears to confirm widely held, preexisting notions of relevant character flaws, a single incident can overturn a career of accomplishment.

Inevitably, even the most adept candidates slip. They commit "gaffes." The most damaging are those that appear to reveal or confirm their innermost thinking—and how it departs from their methodically nurtured public image.

Given the workings of the Special Interest State, it is perhaps not surprising that some of the most memorable gaffes occur at fundraising events. Could it be that candidates are liable to let their guard down among those with whom they feel the greatest kinship?

Thus Barack Obama made a notorious statement to wealthy supporters in San Francisco in 2008. Referring to heartland voters, he said:

> It's not surprising then they get bitter, they cling to guns or religion or antipathy toward people who aren't like them or anti-immigrant sentiment or anti-trade sentiment as a way to explain their frustration.

Thus Mitt Romney made a notorious statement to wealthy supporters in Florida in 2012. Referring to his challenge in assembling an electoral majority, he said:

> There are 47 percent of the people who will vote for [President Obama] no matter what. All right, there are 47 percent who are with him, who are dependent upon government, who believe that they are victims, who believe that government has a responsibility to care for them, who believe that they are entitled to health care, to food, to housing, to you name it. That that's an entitlement. And the government should give it to them. And they will vote for this president no matter what. And I mean, the president starts off with 48, 49, 48—he starts off with a huge number...And so my job is not to worry about those people—I'll never convince them that they should take personal responsibility and care for their lives.

Subsequent protestations notwithstanding, it is hard to avoid the conclusion that Obama and Romney were each expressing their unvarnished views, cocooned and cossetted amid the comforting company of their special-interest sponsors.

Head Fakes

To overcome the appearance of having sold themselves to special interests, a staple of recent presidential campaigns is the "Sister Souljah" moment. This refers to a gesture calculated to persuade mainstream voters that the candidate maintains a degree of independence from the dictates of their legacy party's base.

Bill Clinton pioneered this tactic in his 1992 presidential campaign. He rebuked a theretofore little-known activist known as Sister Souljah for her comment, "If black people kill black people every day, why not have a week and kill white people?"

Clinton, then governor of Arkansas, also evaded being stereotyped as a captive of Democratic Party interest groups by signing off on the execution of Rickey Ray Rector. Rector was reported to be mentally defective, the result of a botched suicide attempt. Poignantly, at the time of his final meal, he asked that his pecan pie be saved "for later."

Clinton, a skilled wordsmith, popularized several locutions intended to imply distance from the dominant interests of his party's coalition. Thus abortion would be "safe, legal—and rare." He would end "welfare as we know it."

George W. Bush followed suit. He spoke of the "soft bigotry of low expectations." He called for a "compassionate conservatism."

Barack Obama offered hope for transcending the divide between "blue" states and "red" states. His biracial background implicitly offered reason to believe that his election would usher in a new political era.

It is difficult to interpret such political moves as anything more than head fakes to the electorate. Each continued to run in lock-step with their special-interest sponsors.

Closing the Aperture of Presidential Vision

One might say that contemporary candidates protest too much. Sister Souljah moments and rhetorical legerdemain cannot obscure the reality that presidential deviations from special-interest dictates are all but extinct.

President Reagan reconfigured the interest-group alignments of his time. Notably, he came to terms with the opposing party to craft a comprehensive tax reform in 1986. He signed comprehensive immigration reform in the same year. In the face of the skepticism and opposition of key supporters, he subsequently crafted historic arms-control agreements with the Soviet Union.

President George H. W. Bush crossed his interest-group coalition in supporting major tax increases as part of a deficit-reduction legislative package. This was an essential element of his failure to achieve reelection.

President Clinton challenged the interest-group alignments of his time, though to a lesser degree. The North American Free Trade Agreement and welfare reform are striking examples.

As the tentacles of the Special Interest State have expanded and tightened, their successors have stayed much more in line. It is difficult to make a convincing argument that George W. Bush or Barack Obama has deviated significantly from their constituent special interests.

Interestingly, some of the greatest errors of the Bush-Obama years were committed amid the constricted space outside of immediate special-interest dictation. For Bush, that would include the decision to commit the United States to war in Iraq. For Obama, that would include at least two decisions relating to health insurance reform: his opting to push it as a first priority, despite the calls to respond to a weakening economy; and his willingness to push such fundamental legislation through Congress on party-line votes.

Are we to be surprised that presidents who emerge from the electoral system of the Special Interest State lack experience in exercising independent judgment?

First the Conventions, Then the Conventional

A presidential candidate who emerges victorious in the legacy-party nomination process has assuredly accommodated himself to a plethora of interest-group expectations and demands. Primaries, caucuses, and endorsements are won at the cost of ever more numerous commitments to special interests.

The familiar spectacle of candidates stumbling over themselves to defend ethanol subsidies in Iowa is not edifying. Witnessing oleaginous politicians declare their perpetual commitment to New Hampshire's first place in the nomination calendar is not inspiring. The pressures of the ongoing demands end up rubbing away interesting aspects that may have occasioned a candidate's initial appeal.

At the party nominating conventions, the victors face one of their defining moments: the selection of a vice president. In modern times, the vice presidency has become highly important. The death or resignation of presidents has too often propelled their running mates into the Oval Office. For others, the second slot has become an unmatched training ground and launching pad for their own presidential aspirations.

Recent vice presidential selections have tended toward individuals who are tightly aligned with their legacy-party interest-group coalitions. Democrat Joe Biden spent his entire career in the US Senate, becoming acculturated to the Special Interest State. Paul Ryan, the 2012 Republican vice presidential nominee, is a career member of the US House. Each possesses an unerring, sincerely held instinct for serving the special interests that hold the greatest sway in their respective parties.

So, too, the legacy-party presidential platforms are crafted with an eye toward governance. Observers tend to dismiss the significance of the platforms. The general public does not focus on these curious documents. They tend to interweave platitudinous sentimentality with discordant, highly specific commitments to narrow constituencies. Their drafting provides a gathering point for interest-group

Understandably, people of talent gravitate toward where they can be most effective. White House staff members can combine lower demands for public accountability with enhanced influence over policy. Few are subject to Senate confirmation and the attendant scrutiny—prompted by affected interests—that bedevils appointees to the agencies.

The episodic interventions of White House staff spawn a vicious cycle. Agency procedures are taken less seriously by all concerned.

Any single White House intervention may serve a particular interest for a specific purpose. At the same time, stripping technical decisions from their larger context can result in incoherence in broader policies. So, too, the degree of roundabout, legalistic reasoning required to conjure up exceptions can occasion additional, unproductive regulatory complexity. This can leave the door ajar to ongoing special interest mischief.

The institutional history and integrity of agencies are being ridden roughshod. White House staff, steeped in the Special Interest State, come to regard departments as little more than treasure boxes for plunder. Rather than assisting and guiding agencies in governance, White House staff tend to represent supportive interests vis-à-vis their presidents' own appointees.

It's a telling sign of the times that a presidential chief of staff would be appointed from the Congress (where he was a point person for special-interest influence in partisan campaigns) and would subsequently depart the White House to seek election as a big-city mayor.

Regulatory Capture 2.0. Concern about "regulatory capture" of federal agencies culminated in extensive reforms in the 1960s and 1970s. They were intended to ensure that federal bureaucracies operate independently of undue industry influence.

Unfortunately, special-interest influence has mutated. Like a resistant virus, it has transformed itself, overtaking prior efforts to create immunity.

For example, the energy and environmental regulatory arena is beset by intense special-interest infiltration. Its situation is representative of broader trends.

Under President George W. Bush, the Environmental Protection Agency was criticized, along with the Department of Interior, for becoming too close to industry. This began at the start, with appointments of individuals to key positions whose primary experience was with highly regulated companies and their lobbying arms. Missteps and scandals were the foreseeable result.

Under President Obama, corresponding criticism was leveled, from another vantage point. On the one hand, there were significant issues of regulatory capture by industry. An example is the favoritism applied by the Department of Energy in subsidizing companies engaged in "pay to play" politics.

The Obama EPA had an additional wrinkle: regulatory capture by environmental advocacy groups. The agency's administrator publicly acknowledged that the agency worked directly with NGOs to draft and earn public support for regulations. This might seem harmless—until one considers that the agency is entrusted to act impartially and independently.

In part this reflects the unwillingness of some special interests to recognize themselves as such. It also illuminates an outdated legal regime relating to conflicts of interest. Industry interest groups are kept at bay by rules limiting agency officials from taking actions in which they have a financial stake. There are no corresponding rules relating to conflicts of interest when officials place a thumb on the scale for nonbusiness interest groups. Thus NGOs, foundations, universities, and others with their own interests are given greater room for maneuver. All the while, public confidence in the system is further compromised.

Government agencies, too, may have their own interests to advance. For example, controversial departments such as the EPA may turn to sympathetic interests to assist in lobbying Congress for their budgets.

You might well say that they should pass a law prohibiting such an obvious conflict of interest. In fact, "they" have: in 1919. Federal statute prohibits agencies from lobbying with government funds.

This brings us to another prominent casualty of the Special Interest State: the historic notion of law enforcement, without fear or favor.

Law enforcement compromised. The first words of the presidential oath include the commitment to "faithfully execute" the laws. This is the essential predicate to a government built on laws rather than the whims of individual officials.

Historically, law enforcement has been understood to be sacrosanct. The ideal of politics stopping at the nation's shores has a corresponding ideal of law enforcement being isolated from political influence.

The Special Interest State is bending law-enforcement independence to the breaking point.

Recent presidents have failed to enforce laws their supporting interests oppose.

Chicanery on Wall Street was exposed in the aftermath of the financial turbulence that began in 2008. No top CEOs were brought to book. In further contrast to the aftermath of the crash of 1929, there was not even a serious effort to replicate the work of the Pecora Senate investigations that laid the groundwork for New Deal reforms.

Immigration law enforcement has been, charitably speaking, sporadic, for years. Had the immigration laws been reliably enforced in recent decades, one imagines that the pressure for reform would have been more focused, more urgent. Instead, the lack of enforcement supports an unsustainable status quo. All the while, public confidence in the legitimacy of government erodes.

There are many more examples. Take a close look at recent disasters in the environmental and public health space. The BP oil spill calamity of 2010 was prefigured by reduced corporate investment in and attention to health and safety. The company had spent years building goodwill and political influence. It had earned the benefit of the doubt from many.

As a result, even in the aftermath of a refinery explosion in Texas in 2005, government officials did not heighten law enforcement sufficiently to push BP back on the straight-and-narrow path. One might have expected a stronger response given that BP had compiled the worst fatality record in the industry in the period from 1995 to 2005.

Consider the recent scandals of the IRS. Political abuse of the taxation authorities has occurred before in our history. It was alleged at various times from the 1930s through the Watergate scandals of the 1970s. In our time of law-enforcement laxity, there is little astonishment at revelations of favoritism for friends and targeting of opponents. Public opinion polls show widespread support for an independent special counsel investigation. Yet there is little real-time pressure of the sort that would prompt a recalcitrant administration into action.

The capture of law enforcement by partisans and special interests is serious enough. Perhaps even more disturbing is the use of law-enforcement powers by government agencies for their own profit. Such corrupt enterprises are special interests working their will behind uniforms and badges.

This is seen in abuses ranging from asset forfeitures to localities adjusting yellow-light times to occasion more violations and higher fines. In some areas, there is systematic abuse of lower-income citizens who run afoul of innumerable laws and regulations and then face astronomical, escalating penalties for nonpayment.

The problem goes straight to the top. Consider the records of recent attorneys general. One courted scandal for political interference in the hiring and firing of US attorneys and other Department of Justice personnel. Another departed to return to his prior law firm. His partners are reported to have maintained his office space throughout his tenure at the Department of Justice. In that memorable, symbolic stroke, they flaunted their influence while assuring their erstwhile colleague of a safe haven.

Is anyone surprised that a 2015 Pew Research poll revealed that only 46 percent of Americans have a favorable impression of the US Department of Justice?

One serious candidate entered the race for the 2016 presidential election while under indictment. Another sought to withhold public information through admitted noncompliance with federal laws relating to record keeping and communication of public officials.

Future generations might well marvel that such candidacies were not summarily rejected.

Opaque decision making. It's become de rigueur for presidential candidates to declare their commitment to transparency in governance. So, too, members of the "out" party seeking to control Congress earnestly promise transparency in operations and legislation.

Time and again these commitments are abandoned in office.

The digital revolution has dramatically increased the capacity of citizens to monitor and participate in governance. At the same time, the special interests who deploy such technologies to their own advantage recognize that transparency is a threat to their dominance. Regrettably, the government has cast its lot with the interest groups, limiting transparency.

Recent administrations have systematically destroyed e-mails and more generally evaded statutory and regulatory record-keeping requirements. Campaign promises—such as proposing that negotiations about major legislation would be open to the public—have been discarded casually.

The Special Interest State operates most effectively in the dark.

The Special Interest State meets the National Security State. President Eisenhower famously warned of the emergence of the "military-industrial complex." In our time, it might be seen as the place where the Special Interest State meets the National Security State. Some have called it the "deep state."

Is it an accident that the apparatus of the National Security State has expanded with each crisis since the end of the Second World War? Weapons systems, military bases, and intelligence-gathering capacities are shielded from transparency and accountability. Without definitions of "success," the wartime footing never ends.

There's no after-action analysis, with public deliberation and understanding, of major defense and foreign policy initiatives.

Edward Snowden's historic breaches of classified information were a reminder that the bureaucracies of the National Security State operate outside of public accountability. They pursue their own organizational interests. Snowden's personal history as a contractor exemplifies the ever-increasing links between the private sector and the defense and intelligence operations of government. This is concerning enough in itself. It is all the more troubling when one considers that many such companies are multinational in scope—and some serve foreign governments.

The longtime abandonment of war powers and oversight authority by the legislative branch means that these defense and intelligence agencies can be directed unilaterally by presidents. The National Security Council is the established management vehicle.

Nonetheless, even the most determined president would have difficulty navigating much less guiding the shape-shifting netherworld comprising the Central Intelligence Agency, the Department of Defense, the Department of Homeland Security, the Department of State, the Federal Bureau of Investigation, the Justice Department, and specialized judicial tribunals.

In recent years a revolving door has been installed between corporate contractors and financial firms and the top officials in this vast, murky, largely unaccountable realm. This door represents the deepening, interlocking connections between the National Security State and the Special Interest State.

The Special Interest State inhibits the evolution of government to meet new challenges. One of the defining characteristics of the Special Interest State is its resistance to necessary change and reform. The inability of government to respond to new challenges, as outlined in chapter 1, is exemplified by organizational inflexibility.

For example, the federal energy and environmental agencies have long been notoriously dysfunctional. So, too, there are outdated programs in other cabinet clusters, such as health-education-welfare. Intelligence and law-enforcement functions are scattered across various agencies and departments. Each of these metastasizing bureaucratic organisms poses additional problems—and is congenial ground for abuse and incompetence—in its interactions with state and local jurisdictions.

Rather than being reordered to serve the public more effectively, an indefensible status quo is rendered inviolate by the combined self-interest of stakeholders. The dysfunction migrates from the executive branch to congressional committee structure and customs. The challenge of effective management, much less reorganization, is so great that presidents increasingly succumb to ad hoc arrangements (such as White House "czars") to achieve high-priority tasks.

Presidency Is the Hub of the Spokes

In theory, the presidency is where the Special Interest State could be mastered. Instead, the special interests are mastering the presidency. The White House has emerged as the headquarters of the Special Interest State.

In turn, this affects the other branches. As we have seen, the Congress is complicit.

So, too, the courts are affected. Special interests have become central to the selection and confirmation of judges. This is among the factors that encourage the public to view the courts as yet another political venue. Many proposals to "reform" the Supreme Court tend to presume it is, for all intents and purposes, a de facto legislature. Thus, for example, a common proposal is to place term limits on justices.

The Supreme Court has unique responsibilities and challenges amid the growth of the Special Interest State. As we have noted, it is increasingly common that controversial statutes are marred by drafting defects. Legal challenges ensue. The Supreme Court is limited by procedural and substantive rules from examining such statutes as a whole. The justices' inquiries are restricted to the evidence and questions arising in the case or controversy before them. Even if they are able to "repair" legally problematic parts of statutes, they may inadvertently disorder the relationship of one part of the law to another.

So, too, the philosophical division of the court, accentuated by the overtly partisan Senate confirmation process, lends itself to split decisions. The rationale for judicial independence and life tenure is difficult to defend in such circumstances.

The Special Interest State, having enmeshed the executive and legislative branches, inevitably touches—and tarnishes—the judicial branch.

Make no mistake: Washington, DC, is under new management.

Can we look to the states for independence from the Special Interest State?

The States and the Special Interest State

For many years there was a safety valve to the emergence of the Special Interest State in Washington: the relative independence of many states and their elected officials.

As a result, the Congress could be roused to significant action through the dedicated leadership of individual legislators. Such members might hail from smaller states or otherwise be less in the thrall of special interests.

Thus the Democrats and Republicans in the Senate were led by notably effective members such as Mike Mansfield of Montana and Howard Baker of Tennessee. Major legislation in areas of special-interest contention and deadlock was achieved by comparatively independent members such as Senators Alan Simpson (immigration reform) and Bill Bradley (tax reform).

Over the course of the past four decades, special interests have become more and more involved in state elections. Small states are often regarded as exceptional "investments." The amount of money required for television, for example, is dramatically less in such states. Wyoming, Delaware, Rhode Island, and Montana have as many senators as California, Texas, Florida, and New York.

As the elections in small states are influenced by special interests of all kinds, the number of operationally independent members is in free fall. When they occasionally emerge, they tend to find themselves isolated in Congress, frustrated by their inability to cobble together coalitions for change.

Special-interest domination in many states has risen to a level comparable to that in Washington. Far from "laboratories of democracy," state governments are, increasingly, adjuncts of the Special Interest State. The first phase of the digital age and social media is accelerating this trend.

The example of California is often offered as a cautionary tale. In the early twentieth century, Hiram Johnson and other leaders liberated state government from the dictation of the railroad trusts and other dominant interests. They introduced innovations such as citizen recall of elected officials and ballot initiatives. Now, those tools have been seized by sophisticated special interests. Many longtime observers view the Golden State as "ungovernable."

As in the United States as a whole, there is remarkably little turnover in the California congressional membership (though the glacier is beginning to crack, with some turnover under the Golden State's new "open," nonpartisan primaries). Statewide office holders tend to be selected from a coterie of career politicians and fundraisers, steeped in the norms of the special-interest culture. At this point, one of the legacy parties dominates all levels of government in California. This reinforces the bias toward the status quo.

The breathtaking result: one of the most innovative areas on earth is governed, at the top rung, by a gerontocracy. This is not to say that individual leaders cannot be effective in their dotage.

Nonetheless, when a cohort of individuals clings to office for decades, backward-looking, reactionary results are not unexpected. Unsurprisingly, their heirs apparent tend to be groomed in their own political image.

Farm Teams

The Special Interest State is mutating to incorporate every level of state officials. Politicians are acculturated into norms of interest-group influence from the start of their careers.

Statewide elected officials are systematically domesticated by interest groups. Consider how such politicians' careers develop. A Democrat may emerge from an NGO or government background. A Republican may emerge from a business or think-tank background. Once elected, they become publicly associated with governance. Almost without reflection, they are assumed by the public and opinion leaders to have relevant experience for higher office.

What is the nature of the experience these individuals obtain?

Consider state elected officials. There is a governor, flanked by a lieutenant governor, attorney general, secretary of state, treasurer/controller, etc.

Twenty-first-century governors are creatures of the Special Interest State. They join national associations that are linked closely to a range of interest groups. This includes legacy-party organizations that raise and disburse campaign funds. It also includes, increasingly, dark money donations from undisclosed sources. Perhaps we should not be surprised that at least one current governor prepared for office through a long career serving special interests as a legacy-party fundraiser and fixer.

Most of the state constitutional offices have few executive functions. The names of their positions may belie their actual roles and responsibilities. For example, state treasurers have little in common with the chief financial officers of companies. Instead, they hold highly circumscribed roles overseeing ongoing bureaucratic operations of state investment. The electoral significance of their tenure is to separate themselves from controversies and associations from their earlier careers, while attaining a platform to speak on budgets, economics, or other public matters.

The day-to-day activities of such state officials vary, state to state and person to person. The commonality is that such offices ensure immersion into the byways and customs of the Special Interest State.

Observe the calendars and phone logs and e-mails of such officials. One tends to find a dense communication network with special interests and legacy-party operatives. The office holders, with few executive responsibilities, devote their time to meeting with and speaking to interest groups that constitute their base of support.

After several years of this, combined with the public platform of their position, such individuals are deemed "qualified" to serve in higher office. Of course, what they are really qualified to do is serve interlocking special-interest and legacy-party networks.

One way such officials earn interest-group sponsorship for higher office is by involving themselves in ballot initiatives. In states such as California and Arizona, for example, statewide candidates routinely head supporting or opposing campaigns around measures of intense concern to their supporters. In an Orwellian flourish, it's not uncommon for politicians to characterize such advocacy as fighting against "special interests."

Is it any wonder that initially well-motivated aspirants are transformed into stewards of the status quo?

The situation of the state attorneys general is unique. Many wield significant authority, with limited accountability to the governor and legislature. They hold fiduciary responsibilities from their independent role as chief law-enforcement officer.

In recent years, national interest groups have systematically engaged state attorneys general. In exchange for current and prospective financial support, attorneys general coordinate with their colleagues in other states, as well as with sympathetic interest groups. Each of the legacy parties has its stable of favored interests; each plays the same game. The National Association of Attorneys General is often referred to as the "National Association of Aspiring Governors."

Within the elasticity of prosecutorial discretion, attorneys general can pick and choose cases that advance the interest groups with whom they are aligned. Republicans tend to favor business interests. Democrats tend to favor labor and consumer interests.

What is increasingly lost is public confidence in the independence of the legal system built around notions of justice, blind to position or power, without fear or favor.

In theory, one might look to other state offices to operate as circuit breakers when attorneys general whiff on their enforcement responsibilities. In fact, just as special-interest infestation has disordered the relationship between the branches of the national government, so, too, it is working its will in the states.

Governors hold an array of formal and informal authorities relating to law enforcement. Regrettably, as presidents have suborned their law-enforcement authorities to special interests, their example is being emulated by their counterparts in the states.

A striking incident in Arizona is emblematic. A new governor suspended enforcement of a state regulatory statute. He simultaneously announced the firing of the appointive official in charge. There was no question that the appointee served at the pleasure of the governor. The problem was that rather than change the statute, the governor unilaterally overrode the law. Astonishingly, the governor publicly touted his abuse of process as "legal reform."

With the blinding absence of self-awareness emblematic of Special Interest State functionaries, the same governor publicly criticized the failure of the president to strictly enforce federal laws on immigration and health care.

So, too, there has been encroachment on state regulatory entities that are constitutionally established as independent of special-interest influence.

In California and Arizona, for example, utilities are sequestered from political activity by a dense ecosystem encompassing state constitutions, statutes, regulations, and longstanding customs. The influence, structure, and reach of regulated utilities make this at once manifestly necessary and entirely feasible.

Nonetheless, the Special Interest State has infiltrated the supposedly sacrosanct regulatory process. In California, a former utility executive who served on the Public Utilities Commission engaged in clandestine negotiations with his erstwhile colleagues. This reportedly included sharing enforcement-sensitive information.

In Arizona, sitting members of the Corporation Commission have been exposed as engaging in extensive, ex parte communications with representatives of the state's largest utility. This reportedly includes communication with dark money operations supporting sympathetic candidates for election to the regulatory commission itself. In addition, dark money from the state's largest utility was reportedly directed to a statewide campaign of a family member of a sitting commissioner.

Dark money, believed to be from the same utility, also poured into the campaigns of the winning candidates for attorney general and governor. This was presumably intended to create a fail-safe mechanism, protecting the utility's "investment" in the commission from unwelcome interference.

With the government under the influence of regulated parties, it falls upon NGOs and concerned citizens to force transparency. There is good news in the Arizona case: A Washington, DC–based not-for-profit is working to hold state officials to account.

There is also disturbing news: the "good guys" seeking transparency are themselves affiliated with a dark-money organization. It appears to be financed by donations from companies and other interest groups who disagree with the Corporation Commission's regulatory decisions.

The tentacles of the Special Interest State infiltrate further and further into the minutiae of governance. More and more gubernatorial appointees and state legislators are swept into its embrace. Interest groups reach them through networks of educational foundations and think tanks that inculcate ideology while they share policy ideas and "best practices" from other jurisdictions.

The encroachment of the Special Interest State has clear implications for the policies proposed and implemented in the states. At least as important for the future, it signals a "new normal" for politicians, beginning at the lowest rungs of the ladder, reaching all the way to the White House.

Consequences of the Special Interest State

Some people, confronted with the realities of the Special Interest State, are fatalistic. They believe that politics has always been—and always will be—an area of compromised ethics. They are resigned to Washington operating as in *House of Cards*—but without the competence.

Bismarck is quoted to the effect that one does not want to see laws or sausages being made. Perhaps it is akin to what goes on in many great hotels. The front lobby and other common areas are extraordinarily beautiful, ordered, clean, warm, and welcoming. Behind the scenes, the kitchen may be chaotic; the catering and delivery areas may be another thing altogether. And yet, most people never see behind the scenes.

In politics, the stakes are infinitely higher. Rising, often involuntary transparency is enabling us to see more than ever before. There is good, and there is bad. There's no responsible option to claim it does not matter.

As we have seen, the Special Interest State has a number of significant consequences:

Consent of the governed is manufactured. As Lincoln urged, the essence of the American experiment is that legitimate government power is derived from the consent of the governed. In the Special Interest State, consent is manufactured. Special interests, operating through the shells of subsidized and protected legacy-party organizations, unduly influence the selection and decisions of politicians. Democracy is suborned. Citizenship is degraded.

The status quo is protected. The American constitutional system of government is intended to discourage abuse of power. This is a natural outgrowth of its creation in our war for independence from English rule. The result is an institutional bias toward the status quo, a ballast to an extraordinary experiment in representative governance.

Today, by any measure that matters, the United States is the leading world power. At home, the federal government reaches into all aspects of national life. Special interests, who pluck privileges from government, can become an immutable force for inertia.

Many interests monetize their involvement with the current structure of governance. They obtain financial gain from the favorable drafting of statutes and regulations. So, too, they profit from governmental structures and rules that afford them special access and relationships.

As a result, they become de facto guardians of existing institutions and customs, even when they are woefully out of date or dysfunctional.

This trend is exacerbated by other factors. In some cases, the rationale for government action is defined such that the mission has no clear end point ("war on poverty," "war on drugs," etc.). Or, as the missions of agencies evolve (e.g., the Department of Labor, Department of Agriculture, Environmental Protection Agency, etc.), outdated governmental statutes and structures remain intact.

Regulated sectors are shielded from competition, innovation. Several of the most important areas of national life are regulated extensively. Examples include finance, health care, transportation, energy, and environment and safety.

In the Special Interest State, such vital sectors are often shielded from innovation as various actors obtain competitive advantage through statutes and regulations. Established enterprises and networks have an immense structural advantage against newcomers.

By contrast, disruptive enterprises line up against entrenched political power. They have no choice but to become involved in the political bazaar if they would serve on a large scale. The added costs can delay or limit their capacity to break through to consumers. Should they run the gauntlet and achieve success in the political realm, they may decide they have a stake in perpetuating the system.

Division is institutionalized. The Special Interest State conjoins the rise of special interests with the protected, unexamined status of the legacy-party duopoly.

Two-way partisan conflict is the vehicle by which special interests seek primacy. This feeds naturally into the widespread tendency to see the world in binary terms of either/or, good and evil, right and wrong. Compromise is discouraged.

Elections are, necessarily, zero sum. One side wins, one loses. Yet it is not necessary that politics itself be zero sum. We have been conditioned to accept it as "normal."

The Special Interest State institutionalizes division. Interests express their views and goals through the either-or, take-it-or-leave-it offerings presented by the legacy parties. The Democrats and Republicans offer half-truths—and are unable to address the whole picture.

Consider some of the staples of today's politics. Highly negative political campaigns are the new normal. They focus on the unsuitability of the opposing candidate. Political rhetoric is overheated. Advocates catastrophize the consequences that would ensue, should their favored campaigns lose. Interest groups resist even the most limited concessions, pointing toward an inevitable slippery slope.

Partisan division has become reflexive. The results can be absurd.

Anything that partisans on one side support, partisans on the other will oppose. Attention to and analysis of policy questions is, all too often, lost amid torrents of vitriol. Effective or popular policies are routinely discarded or repackaged when one of the legacy parties succeeds the other into office. As one would expect, the capacity of government institutions to improve performance and earn public support is degraded.

Such negative campaigning is a great boon to the status quo. It diverts public attention from underlying questions that might be discomfiting or threatening to dominant interest groups. It can also be an incentive for campaigns to discourage participation of likely voters for their opponents. Following the intensely negative campaign of 2012, it is not an accident that Barack Obama emerged as the sole president of the modern era to be reelected with fewer votes than in his initial victory.

False framing of issues. The Special Interest State has so beclouded the scene that major, relevant policy issues are shielded from public debate.

For example, reform of the individual and corporate tax systems is repeatedly delayed. Numerous interests, seeking advantage, remove obvious questions from consideration. Any reconsideration of the mortgage interest deduction, a clear subsidy to wealth, is rendered a "poison pill" by the all-powerful National Association of Realtors.

To raise such issues is to confront the entrenched power of reactionary interests that resist informed public discussion. Prospective innovations, such as taxes on pollution (e.g., carbon) to replace taxes on value creation (e.g., income and payroll taxes), are relegated to debating societies, academia, and good-government forums of retired officeholders.

Various policy questions are deadlocked because of the false choices dictated by special interests. Consider, for example, the proposed Keystone Pipeline, a longtime point of contention between environmental advocates, energy companies, labor unions, state and local governments, the US Department of State, Canadian stakeholders, and a passel of exceptionally wealthy individuals. It is generally understood to be an all-or-nothing proposition.

A highly accomplished public citizen not beholden to the interest groups presented additional options. Billionaire Michael Bloomberg proposed that the American and Canadian governments negotiate an agreement to allow construction of the pipeline while simultaneously limiting greenhouse gas emissions by a significantly greater amount than the project would have occasioned. The result would have been a net positive for the environment and affected industry and unions.

Absent the Special Interest State occupation of Washington, one would anticipate that the president, legislators, institutional stakeholders, and ordinary citizens could come up with any number of such creative approaches to any number of vexing issues. Instead, Bloomberg's suggested approach was orphaned.

How many other creative ideas languish and die in the inhospitable terrain of the Special Interest State?

Outdated, inflexible interest-group coalitions limit political choices of citizens. As we have noted, the legacy parties, the Democrats and Republicans, have declined into little more than subsidized, privileged vessels through which special interests operate. The so-called two-party system is not subject to meaningful competition from third parties and independents. As a result, the interest-group coalitions within each party become entrenched. The alliances are out of date and out of sync. Differences with the other legacy party are exaggerated to harden the coalitions' veneer of relevance and urgency.

This disserves the public. We are forced to choose between prefabricated slates of issue positions that we may find unpalatable. They are certainly not inevitable.

If I am a voter, for example, who seeks greater environmental protections, I may tend toward the Democrats. If, at the same time, I seek greater fiscal responsibility, I may tend toward the Republicans. I may distance myself from the quandary by registering as an independent. Yet that does not advance the combination of issues that I believe are most important. In the short term, the movement out of the legacy parties exacerbates the problem, as the remaining base voters in each party become more ideologically monochromatic.

New, updated coalitions are strangled in the crib.

There are manifest areas of shared concern, for example, between environmental advocacy groups and evangelical voters. So, too, there are commonalities between the right-leaning Tea Party and the left-leaning Occupy movements. The prospect of such reconfigured alliances could offer citizens more ways to inform and express our values. However, such change would destabilize longstanding arrangements favored by functionaries and beneficiaries of the Special Interest State.

We are left with the equivalent of being forced to choose 1960s record albums rather than iPods. The content is selected by others and offered to us as a take-it-or-leave-it proposition. One is compelled to purchase ten songs one cannot abide just to get the one that has spawned an earworm.

We can now curate our musical collections. Our political choices remain archaic: analog offerings in a digital age. Special interests are deciding what will be offered to us. They are blocking our capacity to guide our own government.

Inputs are the focus; outputs are overlooked. When we say we want government to operate more like a business, we are calling for accountability. Good business practices focus on the bottom line, on outputs. We focus on results.

By contrast, politicians focus on inputs. They avoid committing to specific metrics for evaluating results of programs. They feel that their job is done when a law is passed, when a program is funded.

Is it any wonder that we simply accrete more and more programs, piled one on another?

Undue influence by special interests exacerbates this tendency. They define success by what they obtain for themselves in legislation and regulation. The "outputs" they seek are inputs into the governing process. In turn, congressional oversight and investigations are often misdirected or discouraged.

The public interest is advanced by a relentless focus on outputs and accountability. By contrast, the Special Interest State retains a focus on inputs rather than results.

Regulatory Capture 2.0. As we have seen, government officials and agencies are frequently captured by special interests they are intended to regulate. Rather than serve the public in whose name they exist and operate, they become allied with various interest groups. To be sure, they do not tend to recognize themselves in this tableau. They may presume that they are aligned with the public interest.

Such public agencies not only ally with selected interests; they, too, may operate as interests. They may enter coalitions with other privileged organizations and individuals to protect their own resources.

Costs of compromise placed on the backs of future generations. The Special Interest State undermines the animating purpose of any effective democratic republic: serving future generations.

It is not an accident that the rise of the Special Interest State has occurred in tandem with the explosive increase of public debt. As our politics has deadlocked, compromises are achieved by placing burdens on those who are not present. With more and more stakeholders participating in the Special Interest State, there is a relentless tendency to shift costs to future generations.

This dysfunction can be seen not only in fiscal terms, but in debts being incurred through environmental and energy risks, for example.

Individual officeholders are of less consequence. The ideal officeholders of the Special Interest State are not selected for their independent cast of mind, their dedication to governing per se. Regnant interests seek representatives who will robotically execute their agenda.

The desire for candidates who will "shut up and toe the line" fits well with political campaigns that are highly negative, tearing down opponents. This helps camouflage the operations of the underlying interests. It also discredits the process and lowers the caliber of prospective candidates.

This can be obscured by the emergence of so-called "identity politics." Many citizens are persuaded that personal aspects of candidates are decisive. The Special Interest State benefits from this perspective. The fact that an individual officeholder is male or female, of this or that mixture of races and ethnicities, of one generation or another, will be viewed by some voters as consequential in itself.

From the point of view of the Special Interest State, this amounts to rotating the actors. All the while, the writers, directors, and producers ensure that the show goes on.

There are occasional exceptions in presidential campaigns. Candidates may emerge, for a time, who are refreshing in their independence from conventional politics. They're outspoken, brash, willing to say what's what. Not having not come up through the system, they talk about issues in language that has not been pounded into pablum. However, such candidates have tended to fall as quickly as they rise. To date, the Special Interest State has prevailed.

Elections' impact limited. Elections are the ultimate exercise of citizen sovereignty. Increasingly, Americans do not believe that they make a difference.

The millions of us who think that are right.

Consider the 2008 election. Barack Obama promised a resurgence of civil liberties. He would roll back provisions of the Patriot Act. He would rein in the warrantless wiretaps of the National Security Agency.

After two terms, these and other national security policies remain largely intact. The National Security State and the Special Interest State combine to protect the status quo.

Consider the 2014 election. Congressional Republicans were swept in on a wave of discontent with a Democratic president. A major theme was to challenge politics as usual.

What did we find in the aftermath of this electoral earthquake?

Within days, the legacy parties in Congress joined to pass budget legislation that included the customary buffet of special-interest concessions. These included marquee items such as major increases in donor limits for the legacy parties; alterations to the Dodd-Frank financial regulatory scheme; curtailing the sovereignty of the District of Columbia to legalize marijuana, etc.

As so often in the Special Interest State, many of these provisions were crafted outside of public view. Senior politicians, who could have derailed the process, chose to support the package to obtain benefits for favored interests. Some publicly distanced themselves from the results as a whole, while claiming credit for the bits they wished to be associated with.

In the Special Interest State, it seems that all candidates are incumbents; none are insurgents. The only difference is which group of claimants they will favor.

An entitlement ethic pervades the system. Who would have thought that America, founded in a revolution against monarchy and aristocracy, would foster family dynasties in national politics?

As the 2016 election season opened—in 2015—the top tier of presidential contenders included members of the Bush and Clinton families. This is the ultimate manifestation of the oligarchic tendencies and status quo orientation of the Special Interest State. Should just one of them attain their respective party's nomination, it would be the ninth time since 1980 that a member of these two families was on a national political ticket.

The dead hand of the past is holding on to the steering wheel, with no intention of letting go.

Reflecting on where we are, it is worth asking: *What would the founders say?*

As revolutionaries, they might well wonder why we would resign ourselves to our present circumstances. If our elections no longer disturb the status quo, our task is to disrupt politics.

Fortunately for us, they designed and bequeathed a constitutional system that is a remarkably good fit for the challenges and opportunities of twenty-first-century America.

If we decide to put it to use, we could respond to the founders: *We've got this.*

Disrupt Politics

The Special Interest State

Theme

The Special Interest State has supplanted and subverted our constitutional government. It reaches into all three branches of the federal government, as well as the states.

Elements

- The operating system of the Special Interest State includes the legacy-party duopoly and the rise of a professional political class.
- The Congress
- The President
- The States
- The Special Interest State has distorted various aspects of our politics and government, with real-time consequences for citizens.

A number of the foundations of the Special Interest State arose from twentieth-century workarounds of constitutional provisions. In the new circumstances of the twenty-first century, various constitutional provisions and assumptions are ripe for rediscovery and renewed application.

The Spirit of '08 by Udo Keppler. *Puck,* 1907

Three

A Twenty-First-Century Declaration of Independence

Let me now take a more comprehensive view, and warn you in the most solemn manner against the baneful effects of the spirit of party generally... This spirit, unfortunately, is inseparable from our nature, having its root in the strongest passions of the human mind. It exists under different shapes in all governments, more or less stifled, controlled, or repressed; but in those of the popular form it is seen in its greatest rankness and is truly their worst enemy.

—George Washington, Farewell Address

Every government... is perpetually degenerating toward corruption, from which it must be rescued at certain periods by the resuscitation of its first principles, and the re-establishment of its original constitution.

—Samuel Johnson

There are three widespread approaches to responding to the ongoing crisis in American governance:

Accept the status quo. The legacy parties support the status quo. To be sure, they publicly acknowledge some problems.

How could they not?

Time and time and time again, the party holding power tends to find virtues in aspects of the system that advantage them. By contrast, the out party tends to be more critical. When the cycle turns, their critique tends to dissipate. So, too, it is with various interest groups in coalitions within the legacy parties. The political class based in Washington, DC, tends to favor tangential adjustments that would benefit themselves—invariably safeguarding the essentials of the status quo.

Demand constitutional reform. When their frustration reaches a tipping point, some advocate surgery on the Constitution. It can be amusing to imagine oneself as a twenty-first-century Madison or Franklin or Jefferson or Adams. It is not likely. The Constitution includes amendment provisions that hold just as much force as any others. Nonetheless, with their hard-earned mistrust of precipitate action by government officials and transitory majorities, the founders made amendment difficult. Currently, with the federal government in protracted stalemate, the challenge is all the more daunting.

The bottom line: to propose constitutional change—without more—is to sustain the status quo for the foreseeable future.

Focus on symptoms. Common proposals for change focus on symptoms rather than the underlying system, the Special Interest State. For example, some observers urge a constitutional amendment to overturn the Supreme Court's decision in the *Citizens United* case (holding that corporate, union, and not-for-profit advocacy during political campaigns is protected by the freedom-of-speech guarantee of the First Amendment).

Such an amendment might or might not match the hopes and fears of advocates and critics. What we do know is that the Special Interest State was in full bloom before 2010 and *Citizens United.* There is little reason to think its essential character would be altered solely by reversal of one judicial decision.

Restore Constitutional Government

There is a fourth approach: undertaking major reform within our existing constitutional system. This means making full use of powers and potential that can be achieved now, without self-indulgently longing for chimerical constitutional amendments.

In sum: don't change the Constitution to accommodate our broken politics; instead, change our politics to faithfully follow the Constitution.

This approach holds significant advantages:

- It can be achieved rapidly.
- It retains the two centuries of wisdom and experience embedded in our Constitution.
- It does not preclude simultaneous or sequential efforts to amend the Constitution. The ongoing process of reform can clarify issues and engage the public imagination.

A Glance Back to the Turn of the Twentieth Century

What is to be done? How can we break the death grip of the Special Interest State? How can We the People recover our power over those who govern in our name? How can we ensure that our public servants actually serve us? How can we take action rapidly, meeting the unremitting demands of global leadership in a new century?

The United States is the world's oldest continuously operating democratic republic. Among the benefits of this durability is a vast store of historical experience. We are not the first generations to face fundamental questions of governance at the turn of a new century.

The early twentieth century is often misremembered as a simpler, tranquil time. This is far from apt. It reflects a presumptuous "presentism."

Many Americans of that time were, to be sure, highly optimistic about the future. They were also keenly aware that our governance was under severe stress. They were experiencing and anticipating fundamental change.

Consider American history from the Civil War of the 1860s, through the assassination of Lincoln and the stillborn Reconstruction, and then the Gilded Age of industrial and financial innovation. It was a time of dramatically increasing national wealth, technological advancement, and social and political innovation and turbulence.

Laissez-faire government was a precondition of the explosive development of the Gilded Age. It was, however, increasingly insufficient to deal with a growing roster of destructive consequences.

This set the stage for the Progressive Era. The period from 1890 to 1920 encompasses the political expression of rising demands to reconcile our national values with the industrial age. It includes the unprecedented challenges posed by the First World War and its aftermath.

Many progressive thinkers saw the legacy of the Constitution as incompatible with the needs of an emerging global power. As Herbert Croly wrote in 1914 in his seminal work, *The Promise of American Life,* "The best that can be said on behalf of this traditional American system of political ideas is that it contained the germ of better things."

Croly's viewpoint resonated widely. An overarching theme emerged: the power of centralized government could be transformative—an unprecedented, untapped force for good.

Theodore Roosevelt, Woodrow Wilson, and other leading progressive political figures disagreed vehemently on many issues. Nevertheless, they shared faith in the capacity of the national government to drive progress. A practical necessity was to identify and empower "disinterested" experts who would provide direction to the nation. Governance, in this view, was evolving into a scientific, technocratic enterprise. The citizenry would be best served by aggregating information and drafting policies that would be, objectively, beneficial.

Recall the context of those times. At the dawn of the twentieth century, a single corporate enterprise boasted a capitalization greater than the entire federal government budget. The fundamental debate was between conservatives who rationalized the power and place of organized capital and industry, versus progressives and socialists who sought to restrain the abuses of capital and industry through countervailing forces of government and labor.

One of the most influential thinkers of the time was Frederick Winslow Taylor. Taylor originated the field of industrial management. He applied data-driven analysis to rationalize workplace practices. The underlying assumption was that resources could be most efficiently applied when directed from the top. Workers were regarded as fungible factors of production. The ideal of "Taylorism" was to determine "the one best way" to direct individuals to create value for all. Reposing power in the few would advance the interests of the many.

Taylor's assumptions were widely shared. The progressive approach to governance was constructed on the same world view.

The centralizing tendencies that began in industry would move to government, gathering momentum through much of the twentieth century. Technological and political changes came together in a mutually reinforcing interplay. Two world wars, the Great Depression, and the Cold War accelerated these trends.

Spectacular national capacities were unleashed through government power, directed from Washington, DC. A milestone was the extraordinary military production that Franklin Roosevelt orchestrated during the outset of American participation in the Second World War. A nation with a relatively limited military-industrial capacity transformed itself, with breathtaking speed, into "the arsenal of democracy."

The same impulse was validated in the enactment of a social safety net based largely on European antecedents. So, too, federal power was an indispensable force for good in overcoming state and local politics that heretofore deprived African-Americans and others of their rightful place in national life.

It is no accident that Theodore Roosevelt, Woodrow Wilson, and Franklin Roosevelt chafed under the "straitjacket" of a Constitution conceived in the eighteenth century. It seemed like a horse-and-buggy affair in an age of automobiles, airplanes, industrial war machines, and moon shots.

It was in this ecosystem that the Special Interest State emerged. The constitutional workarounds of twentieth-century politicians inadvertently opened up spaces that would be commandeered by various special interests. The result is a system that is far from the "disinterested" enterprise envisioned in the heady days of the early twentieth century.

A Constitution Designed for the Twenty-First Century

In the twenty-first century, Taylorism is but a distant memory. The notion of "the one best way" is relegated to the dustbin of history. The digital age empowers and connects individuals as never before.

Enterprises are, increasingly, ad hoc networks that create value from the bottom up, from the outside in.

Theodore Roosevelt credibly compared his administration's public management with the best of the private sector. A century later, government and politics are ossified. They are outliers, stubbornly resistant to the disruption unlocking value in sector after sector.

It is fortunate for us that many aspects of the Constitution that many saw as antiquated in the twentieth century have renewed relevance in the twenty-first.

Consider the foundations of the Constitution of 1789:

- dispersed information and power
- skepticism of centralized authority
- protection of individual rights as a precondition of the advancement of the commonwealth
- reliance on citizen sovereignty as the ultimate source of government legitimacy

What Would the Founders Say?

If the American founders were transported into our nation today, what would they think?

They might surprise us with their capacity to comprehend our circumstances. We are living the evolving actualization of principles they engraved into our national life.

One imagines that some things might surprise and concern them.

When did Washington, DC, come to resemble a seat of empire? How did the national financial center—New York—come to have such influence over the seat of government in distant Washington? How did political parties become legally protected and subsidized into a durable duopoly? How did special interests attain such extraordinary power, breaching each of the separate branches of the federal government?

The founders might well note that none of these outcomes was foreordained by the Constitution.

Bring Down the Twin Pillars of the Special Interest State

The Special Interest State rests on two interconnected foundations: the legacy-party duopoly and the rise of a class of "professional" elective politicians.

If we are to break free from the Special Interest State, we must disrupt both elements.

End the Legacy-Party Duopoly

As we become habituated to circumstances and institutions, we are liable to assume that they represent the natural order of things.

So it is with "the two-party system." How often one hears this phrase spoken with a reverent finality. Many presume that it is part of the constitutional framework.

It's past time to end this destructive myth.

There is no constitutional provision for special privileges for the legacy parties. To the contrary, their ongoing duopoly runs afoul of various constitutional provisions.

All too often, the Republicans and Democrats seek to tweak the system around their self-serving needs. The legacy parties are nothing more than legal vessels by which special-interest demands are "laundered" to influence politics with a patina of principle. Serving citizens is, at most, an afterthought.

Why, for example, should citizens be forced by government to subsidize partisan primaries? Is it right that Democrats and independents are compelled to pay taxes that are directed to Republican primaries? Or that Republicans and independents should be conscripted to pay for Democratic primaries?

Having subsidized partisan primaries, can it be right that citizens are nonetheless barred from voting in them? The legacy parties are eager to take your hard-earned money, yet would prevent you from voting in their primaries—unless you submit to endorsing them, registering as a member of their party.

Is it right that Democrats and Republicans use their dominant position to impose differential, disabling ballot access requirements on third parties or nonpartisan candidacies?

Is it right that election regulatory bodies serve the interests of the legacy parties? The Federal Election Commission is statutorily mandated to have six members. No more than three can represent either of the legacy parties. The working presumption is that there will be three Republicans, three Democrats. The inevitable result is paralysis, punctuated by spasms of self-serving activity. Are we to be surprised that partisan appointees do not reflect the American electorate, now including far more independents than members of either legacy party? The commission is structured to protect the partisan status quo from disruption.

Is it right that the legacy parties in many states are the organizing entities for drawing up legislative districts? Why should politicians be empowered to select their own constituents?

Is it acceptable that the legacy parties schedule elections around their self-interest? When it suits their special-interest sponsors, they routinely set votes at times that ensure that turnout will be favorable. This is also a budgetary drain. Tax dollars could be saved by combining elections on a single day.

Rather than have We the People serve the legacy parties, the parties should serve us.

If we are to have a two-party system, it should be because the two parties—and, possibly, others—have competed and we have ratified their status in elections.

There are a number of reforms that can be taken now:

Remove subsidies and other legal privileges of the legacy parties. The First Amendment requires that there be no establishment of religion. Just as surely, those freedoms must override the establishment of a political-party duopoly.

A guiding principle should be: Citizens should not be compelled by government to subsidize political organizations.

In the meantime, to the extent that party primaries are financed by taxpayers, such primaries should be open to all voters.

Other privileges are interspersed throughout various laws and regulations and customs.

An egregious example is the structure of the presidential debates. They are controlled by a bipartisan Commission on Presidential Debates. To be sure, the CPD declares itself "nonpartisan." In fact, it is emblematic of the rampant entitlement of the legacy-party duopoly. It's indicative that former president Bill Clinton serves as cochairman—even as his spouse seeks the presidency in her own right (the former presidents Bush do not hold the role, so the issue does not arise in respect of the candidacy of Jeb Bush).

The commission has crafted a seamless catch-22. To participate in the presidential debates, candidates must demonstrate that they are on the ballot in a sufficient number of states to reach an Electoral College majority and that they have attained 15 percent in national polls.

As journalist and former undersecretary of state James Glassman points out, unless candidates can get into the debates—or have a credible chance of getting in—it's all but impossible for them to overcome those barriers to entry.

Another impediment to a free political marketplace is ballot access. Examples include recent changes in Arizona law to increase the numbers of signatures required for third parties to be included on the ballot. This was sponsored and enacted by Republican majorities with the express purpose of excluding Libertarian candidates. Republicans blamed Libertarians for the loss of several high-profile elections to Democrats.

Another unjustifiable limitation on citizen sovereignty is the widespread adoption of "sore loser" laws. These provisions bar a candidate defeated in a party primary from running under another banner in the general election. In a time of increasing voter registration as independents, such limitations are pernicious. An election campaign should, ideally, be a process in which voters and candidates communicate, each side learning and evolving. Sore-loser laws short-circuit that process. The beneficiaries are the legacy parties and their special-interest masters.

In sum, all legal privileges for the legacy parties should be removed.

Legislative district maps should serve voters, not the legacy parties. Under the Constitution, states hold immense power in drawing district maps for the US House and state legislatures. This is, necessarily, a zero-sum game with real-time consequences for elected officials and the citizens they serve.

All too often, the Democratic and Republican parties have taken control of the redistricting process. Not surprisingly, they craft districts favoring the party in power.

The problem of "gerrymandering" is not new. It began almost as soon as the United States was established. The term originally referred to state senate districts drawn up in Massachusetts in 1812. A cartoonist's pen conveyed what the politicians were up to. One of the districts approved by Governor Elbridge Gerry resembled a salamander in its elongated, curved appearance. The new district consolidated voters who reliably supported the governor's party.

This unedifying practice has persisted through American history. The Democrats employed it to great effect, protecting House majorities from the 1930s into the 1980s. In recent years, the Republicans have exercised the same power to safeguard their legislative majorities.

The application of digital technology has unleashed a level of sophistication previously unimagined. One curiously drawn district in Maryland has been compared to "blood spatter from a crime scene." Communities of geography, history, and interest are routinely overridden as a partisan privilege.

This can result in elections where the party with the larger number of votes cast nonetheless wins fewer House seats. It also enables Democrats and Republicans to disperse independent voters. Given that redistricting generally occurs every ten years, in conjunction with the US Census, the electoral stakes are high.

Several states have sought to curtail such abuses by establishing nonpartisan redistricting commissions. This is a positive trend for citizen sovereignty that should be encouraged for all jurisdictions.

Remove congressional practices based on partisan advantage. George Washington and other founders were skeptical of the emergence of political parties. The Constitution does not expressly contemplate parties. The durability of the subsequent "two-party system" has caused some to overlook partisan overlays that throw congressional operations off course.

A recent example is the so-called "Hastert Rule." Named for a disgraced former congressman, it requires that a majority of the majority party approve of legislation prior to opening it to a vote of the entire House. As intended, this hobbles prospects of bipartisan coalitions in the House of Representatives.

The filibuster might be included in this category. This is a Senate rule that enables an individual member or small group to delay legislative action. The filibuster can be overcome by a cloture vote by three-fifths of the members (sixty votes).

Once a rarity, the filibuster has become the norm. The practical effect is that the constitutional requirement of majority rule has been overturned in favor of a sixty-vote supermajority. This greatly increases the leverage of the minority party in the Senate—and their special-interest patrons.

Even without the filibuster, the constitutional design establishes the Senate as a brake on evanescent public enthusiasms. The six-year term and the equality of membership by state, without regard to population, are anti-majoritarian. The filibuster goes an additional step, constituting an often insurmountable bias in favor of the status quo.

As recounted by congressional reformer Michael Golden, the routine use of the filibuster is inconsistent with the constitutional framework. It should be reexamined and reformed.

Ensure that campaign-finance regulation does not protect the status quo. Following the Watergate scandals of the early 1970s, the United States has implemented a series of campaign-finance reforms intended to combat corruption. Regrettably, the resulting regime tends to reflect and reinforce the status quo.

Our current "system" of campaign financing is, from the point of view of citizens, incoherent. It incents large donors but not small donors. It encourages campaign-related activity outside of official campaigns by autonomous entities not covered by contribution limits. More and more donations are funneled through opaque, dark money organizations. It's safe to assume that most if not all such anonymous donors are well known to the politicians who benefit from their largesse. Candidates are ever more reliant on special interests operating apart from their official campaign organizations.

The current campaign-finance regime is the product of forty years of interactions between politicians, courts, regulatory agencies, and special interests. We can now discern a repeating pattern:

- The politicians in Congress and the White House enact campaign-finance laws.
- The courts are asked to sort out conflicts between the limits on free expression in campaigns and First Amendment protections.

- The judiciary, in its constitutional role, renders judgment on discrete parts of the laws that are involved in specific cases before them. Whatever notions or structures united various statutory provisions are thereby unpacked. This creates additional, practical problems in implementation.
- In response, the politicians continue to tinker. Special interests innovate in ever more creative ways to influence campaigns—and to camouflage their interventions. The electoral regulatory agencies, influenced by the legacy parties, are inert.
- Eventually, a new president and Congress come to terms on a new, "comprehensive" reform package, and the process begins anew.

For all its manifest failings, the campaign-finance system has evolved into a mainstay of the Special Interest State. It may not work for We the People—but it is serving the status quo very well, thank you.

Campaign-finance legislation is inevitably tarnished by immutable conflicts of interest. Republicans and Democrats may view one another with withering contempt. Nonetheless, they share a determination to protect their own interests, including the legacy-party duopoly. They are inclined to craft rule-based systems that codify their advantages.

In this, the political establishment resembles the British military during the American Revolution. The English sought to impose rules of engagement that would reinforce their advantages as the greatest fighting force in the world. By contrast, the Americans refused to be bound by such ground rules. Their insurgency blurred civilian and military lines. As necessity and opportunity arose, they were not reluctant to turn to what we would recognize as guerilla warfare.

The same principles apply to politics. Historic change has been sparked by intensely dedicated platoons of citizens who found ways to bypass the power massed against them. Transformational moments can arise suddenly, at hinge moments.

For example, in 1968, Senator Eugene McCarthy's long-shot insurgency against President Lyndon Johnson was initially financed by a small number of major donors. Such contributions enabled McCarthy's campaign to obtain television time to make his case to the voters of New Hampshire. Absent such seed money, McCarthy could not have assembled the extraordinary coalition that prompted a sitting president to end his reelection drive.

Also in 1968, Alabama Governor George Wallace garnered significant aggregate contributions from a large network of small donors. This represented a milestone in the rising importance of mass participation via direct-mail solicitation.

Today, the Internet offers heretofore unimagined potential for citizen engagement. Several presidential campaigns have gathered large sums from an extensive base of small donors. Yet, even that kind of organization may require seed money from large donors. This may be a practical necessity for insurgencies such as McCarthy's in 1968. When it began, he stood virtually alone, facing down the unified power of a sitting president and the party apparatus.

The Supreme Court, in the landmark case *Buckley v. Valeo* (1976), presented criteria to reconcile post-Watergate campaign-finance regulations with constitutional freedoms. Its terms of analysis remain in place.

In *Buckley*, the court acknowledged the tight nexus of campaign-finance limits and free expression. The Bill of Rights places free speech as the *First* Amendment for a reason. Its text is as unconditional as one could imagine:

> *Congress shall make no law*...abridging the freedom of speech, or of the press; or the right of the people peaceably to assemble,

and to petition the Government for a redress of grievances. [emphasis added]

The Supreme Court stipulated that corruption could result from campaign contributions offered in exchange for specific governmental outcomes. The court also recognized the rights of candidates and independent organizations to express their viewpoints through campaign spending. Transparency in campaign operations was seen as valuable for voters seeking information about candidates, and for enforcement of rules.

Forty years later, the campaign-finance system is dysfunctional in at least three fundamental respects:

The cost of campaigns. As we have seen, the cost of campaigns has become astronomical.

There is a paradox evident in campaign spending in the Special Interest State. The costs of individual campaigns have soared in part because so few elections are competitive. The handful of House contests that are in play receive massive amounts of funding. In presidential elections, a small number of "battleground" states are blanketed with advertising, while other states are overlooked.

Anyone who has endured the 24/7 barrage of political communications in a contested election knows that such spending is, simply, out of control. One aspect is the immense cost of television and radio advertising. Given that these media are publicly licensed, there is every reason to demand that these costs be lowered as a condition of operation. This is, of course, resisted by media companies and many incumbent politicians.

At the same time, the aggregate amount of political spending for the nation as a whole is surprisingly low. The Institute for Justice, citing data from the National Retail Federation, reports that Americans spent far more on Halloween than on the midterm elections of 2014. So, too, more was spent on laundry detergent, pet grooming, tea, and concerts.

An effective campaign-finance system could deal with each of these problems. If more elections become competitive through such changes as gerrymandering reform, the flood of money could be diverted toward a much larger playing field. To enhance the prospect of disruptive change, this could occur while increasing the overall amount of spending relating to political education.

Citizen participation in campaign financing. The *New York Times* reported in 2015 that "158 families provided nearly half of the early money for efforts to capture the White House." There is no more apt illustration of the Special Interest State at work.

There are two general approaches to responding to this development.

The first is for government to continue to ration political expression through limits on contributions and expenditures.

It is not obvious why we should anticipate that this approach would work better in the future than it has in the past. It has created a black market in political activity that is a godsend to special interests.

An alternative approach would be to increase political expression, broadening the base of donors and participants. There are any number of ways this might be done. Tax incentives for small donors, vouchers, and other means might be considered.

In the Internet age, there is immense potential to rouse tens of millions of Americans to participate directly in our politics. We the People are a sleeping giant awaiting our moment. If we are persuaded that we can make a difference, there is reason for optimism.

Absence of public accountability. As with other areas in the Special Interest State, the campaign-finance system operates without actionable public accountability. Reforms to increase transparency and to separate fundraising from lawmaking merit immediate consideration and action (and are described in more detail later in this chapter). Simplifying the current laws and regulations is essential.

Political campaigns are a necessary part of a properly functioning democratic republic. Today, the special interests use campaigns to consolidate their power over public officials. Historically, campaign-finance reform has reflected and reinforced the Special Interest State. We the People should demand that such reforms enlarge our sovereignty over our government.

Competition, not polarization. Many of those who benefit from the status quo will resist reform. This is destructive and irrational, even if foreseeable. It is also self-destructive, if one considers the enlightened self-interest of the Republicans and Democrats.

Today, the legacy parties polarize the electorate in pursuit of power. While they speak of serving the public, their actual focus is serving the special interests who control their organizations. They customarily use negative campaigning, demonizing the opposition to the point of delegitimizing those who are ultimately elected. The citizens to be served are relegated to being little more than an indifferent audience.

We are provided little more than stale talking points from a vanished world.

We the People get it. We are streaming out in record numbers, declaring as independent (or, according to the rules of various states, as "no party preference," etc.).

For all their unjustified privileges, the legacy parties are in a state of advanced, accelerating decomposition. In recent years, the Democrats have lost massive numbers of officeholders at all levels below the presidency. The Republicans are manifestly unable to manage their congressional majorities. American history has no precedent for the peculiar circumstances that rendered the Grand Old Party scarcely able to scare up a Speaker of the House of Representatives in 2015.

As the legacy parties shrink, their resistance to change hardens. The dominion of their constituent interest groups is more crudely asserted. The widely shared but unspoken sense that our current national circumstances are unsustainable encourages all the more short-term, self-centered thinking...The vicious cycle speeds beyond the control of the participants.

The legacy parties are holding a grab-and-run, going-out-of-business sale of our legacy of representative government. We the People should not resign ourselves to codependency.

Fortunately, the basis for a correction is right before us. It is entirely in accord with our constitutional norms.

Consider the decline of the legacy automakers in Detroit. For decades, they sought and received unjustified privileges from politicians in Lansing and Washington, DC. Initially, they were cosseted. Gradually, they succumbed to complacency. Ultimately, they slid toward institutional corruption. They turned, by degrees, from serving consumers to serving politicians, financiers, executives, and labor unions.

This arrangement appeared to be sustainable—for a time. The Big Three lived off the hard-earned trust of a glorious past—and the understandable prejudice of the World War II generation of consumers, who resisted Japanese and German products.

All this worked—until it did not. The absence of competition resulted in inferior products and outdated, self-serving management and labor practices.

When their privileges began to unravel, the automakers faced an existential moment. Their arrangements could not stand. Japanese and German competition changed the game.

There was a happy ending. The American automakers found their footing. They put consumers first. They achieved excellence. They not only restored their relevance; they renewed their just claims of leadership.

In the early twenty-first century, the legacy parties find themselves in a comparable situation. Competition from independent and third-party entities will disrupt them. Ultimately, that disruption will provide an opportunity for the Democrats and Republicans, with their advantages of institutional history, to earn their places.

The Republican and Democratic parties must disrupt or die. Competition is their road to salvation. Vainly striving to maintain the status quo is their road to ruin. As long as they maintain their vise grip on the levers of power, it's also our road to ruin.

Establish Twenty-First-Century Citizen Government

The Special Interest State has risen hand in glove with the centralization of power in Washington in the twentieth century.

Though the results are now dysfunctional, the ideas behind the development were not initially unreasonable. By contrast, the early twenty-first century is marked by decentralization and empowerment of individuals and ad hoc networks. The status quo in Washington, DC, is becoming ever harder to defend.

Create a Citizen Congress. Washington isn't working. We all know it.

The breakdown can be seen vividly in the operations of the Congress. The Constitution establishes the national government on the foundation of the legislative branch. It's not an accident that its role is delineated first, in Article I.

Consistent with the notion of representative democracy, the constitutional vision is one of citizen sovereignty. Stretching across three centuries, members of Congress were citizen legislators. They lived and worked outside the nation's capital. They assembled for limited periods each year.

As the nation's capital rose in prominence in the twentieth century, the tradition of citizen legislators declined. Various arguments were put forward in favor of a "professional" Congress.

It was said that the heightened demands of centralized government required full-time, year-round representatives and senators. Some urged that this would enable Congress to retain its relative power vis-à-vis an ascendant presidency. It was also thought that colocation in Washington would incline individuals to work past partisan divisions. Treating legislative service as a stand-alone, full-time job would elevate its stature and attract strong candidates. Raising salaries and providing pensions would enable members to avoid the conflicts of interest that could arise from pursuing private careers while in public service.

This was an admirable vision. Regrettably, as we have seen, the Special Interest State insinuated itself. A political class has risen in Washington, DC. It is built around the "full-time" Congress. The hopes of earlier times have been dashed.

Given its feeble performance, if we were establishing our federal government today, would we maintain the current operations of Congress? To ask the question is to answer it.

First of all, individual members of Congress are not serving full-time in the sense intended. When they are in session, the members spend inordinate amounts of time raising campaign contributions and otherwise tending to special interests.

A leaked briefing for new members, prepared by the Democratic Congressional Campaign Committee in November 2012, presented the stark realities in a "Model Daily Schedule." In Washington, representatives were urged to have four hours of "Call Time" for contributions; one to two hours for constituent visits; two hours for "Committee/Floor"; one hour for "Strategic Outreach," including "Breakfasts, Meet-and-Greets, Press"; and one hour for "Recharge Time." Corresponding allocations were recommended for time spent in their home districts.

To enable politicians to devote themselves to campaigning for reelection, the Congress curtails the number of days it is actually doing legislative business. For 2016, the House is set to be in session for a mere 111 days. As summarized in the *Washington Post*, "This means the chamber will be closed more weekdays (150) than open, and many of the 111 are partial days. That's upward of 30 weeks of paid vacation for all 435 members of the House."

Second, the Congress has become annexed to the Special Interest State by being co-located in Washington, DC. Members are rapidly acculturated into the ways of the capital. Soon enough, they are assimilated. There's more than a grain of truth in the mordant remark that Congress has become a farm team for K Street lobbying firms.

Beginning anew in the early twenty-first century, we should turn to something more in line with the constitutional vision.

Consider how such a reformed, Citizen Congress might work:

- Members would remain based in their home districts and states. This would keep them grounded. They would share the experiences and concerns of their constituents. Through the Internet, they could simultaneously remain in touch with domestic and world issues. They could gather in digital meetings whenever necessary.
- Members could maintain their private businesses. Why should they not have the option to continue working? Their real-world perspectives would add value in real time. The only

limitations need be conflicts of interest, such as serving as lobbyists during their legislative service. Actionable transparency would be a deterrent to abuse.

- The salaries of members could be reduced accordingly. They could be brought into line with other public-service professions, such as teaching. Based in their home districts, legislators would be spared the challenges of making ends meet in two cities simultaneously. This is particularly difficult in contemporary Washington. Some members of the House have sought refuge from the capital's real estate market by sleeping in their offices.
- Citizen legislators would be expected to live like their fellow citizens. A simple principle could be established: members of Congress and their staffs should follow the same laws and regulations as the citizens they serve. Every law and regulation should be evaluated against this standard.

Regrettably, this is not the case today. Legislators and their staffs are exempted from many of the laws and regulations they enact.

In line with this principle, the congressional pension system should be abolished. Why should our public servants not have the same retirement options as the rest of us? Certainly they should have the same arrangements for health insurance that they have imposed on the rest of us.

Treating members of Congress like other citizens could extend beyond their public service. Former members of the House and Senate now enjoy a series of special privileges open to no one else. Notably, so long as they are not classified officially as lobbyists, they have access to various congressional facilities that put them in proximity with sitting legislators. There is no reason they should not be subject to the same rules as other citizens. It would be just as well if they shuttered their dedicated interest group: the US Association of Former Members of Congress.

- Fundraising could be curtailed within the system that has arisen in Washington. A sensible rule would be to ban all fundraising—by Congress or the president, online or in person—while either house is in session. This would begin to untangle the knotted nexus fusing political fundraising with legislation and regulation.
- Citizen legislators would be well positioned to move from serving special interests to serving their constituents. Freed of ongoing fundraising and located outside of the center of interest-group influence, they could focus more effectively on major issues. From a distance, they would be better able to comprehend the real-world outcomes of legislation. This imparts an entirely different vantage point than attending to the minutiae that are the workaday focus of special interests in Washington. Instead, they could attain the perspective of citizens whose lives and work are affected by laws and regulations. This could equip them for effective oversight of the executive branch, which has been missing for many years.

Defenders of the status quo will offer predictable objections.

Some will say that a "professional" legislature is needed to deal with the complexities of our time. A "part-time" Congress would not be able to keep up.

In fact, as we have seen, members of Congress now serve the American people on a part-time basis. Much of the time that they are actually "working" is consumed with fundraising and other activities relating to special interests.

Others express concern that citizen legislators would be no match for an overweening executive. In fact, the decline of congressional power vis-à-vis the president has accelerated amid the rise of the Special Interest State.

Congress has been blown off course, serving special interests while abdicating its constitutional duties and prerogatives. This includes abandonment of its most fundamental responsibilities: war powers, treaty approvals, budgeting, and executive-branch oversight.

Combined with other reforms, a Citizen Congress would likely reach a new level of diversity, in every sense. Members who more faithfully reflect their districts would bring a range of opinions to their party caucuses. They might also be more diverse in terms of occupation, race, ethnicity, religious affiliation, and gender. Congressional service would become attractive to many who now decline to become career politicians.

Adhering to the constitutional vision would enable Congress to restore its rightful place among the branches of government.

Discarding outdated twentieth-century expectations and approaches can be accomplished without constitutional amendment. Citizen legislators can restore the founders' vision, bringing to bear the extraordinary technological capacities of the twenty-first century.

Match a Citizen Congress with a Citizen Presidency. Changes in the operation of the legislative branch should be matched with corresponding changes in the executive branch. These, too, could be achieved without constitutional amendment.

The ideal of the American presidency was established by George Washington. In a time when classical history was widely studied, Washington emulated and was compared to a legendary Roman general called to the pinnacle of political leadership. Cincinnatus left his farm, accepted the dictatorship during a crisis, and led his nation to victory in war. At the zenith of acclaim and accomplishment, he renounced power, returning to his farm and family.

George Washington is renowned as an historic leader in no small part for his renunciation of power. No one else could have removed "the father of our country" from the presidency. Washington made the unilateral decision to relinquish the reins. He set a high standard for his successors.

In modern times, one thinks of Harry Truman. Truman was called to the presidency following an unlikely confluence of circumstances. A lifelong devotee of history, he held the greatest respect for the institutions and traditions of government.

On the afternoon of his successor's inauguration in 1953, the ex-president, accompanied by his wife, Bess, boarded the train from Union Station back home to Independence, Missouri.

Though he was not entitled to a presidential pension, Truman declined to pursue any business opportunity that was incompatible with his notions of propriety for the nation's "Mr. Citizen." This consigned his family to something close to genteel poverty. Ultimately, a presidential pension was provided, along with office and medical expenses and Secret Service protection.

Truman's values appear otherworldly today. Several recent post presidencies have become, in the words of historian Walter Russell Mead, "post-modern political machines."

The Bush and Clinton families continue to play outsized roles in politics long after their anchor presidencies have ended. The presidential candidacies of Hillary Clinton and Jeb Bush were foreordained. The legacy parties incline to legacy candidacies. The Special Interest State welcomes dynasties; they are seamless status quo succession plans.

Parallel to a reformed Congress, the presidency could be brought into the new circumstances of the twenty-first century:

- The presidential pension could be abolished, in tandem with elimination of congressional pensions. Ex-presidents now have many avenues for moneymaking. Several have become extravagantly wealthy from what is, in effect, a deferred compensation system for former chief executives. Those who would work in not-for-profit enterprises also have many options that were not available to their historical predecessors. There is no reason why presidents should not be limited to the same retirement options as the citizens they serve.

  Some might object that the reform of such privileges would lower the quality of presidential candidates. One need only recall that George Washington, Thomas Jefferson, Abraham Lincoln, Theodore Roosevelt, Woodrow Wilson, and Franklin Roosevelt served effectively as the nation's commander in chief without the inducement of defined benefit pensions and other post presidential perquisites.
- End separate health-care and pension systems for presidential appointees. As with Congress, there is every reason to insist that those executing the laws must live under them. Their lives should be tied, as closely as possible, to those they serve. Presidential appointees—those who serve at the president's discretion—are in temporary positions. They should have the same retirement and health insurance options as their fellow citizens, no more and no less.
- A ban on fundraising while the Congress is in session should extend to the president. This would ensure equilibrium between the legislative and executive branches. It would also be an incentive for both branches to complete legislative sessions as soon as practicable.

Affix Accountability

Public accountability is a casualty of the Special Interest State. The engines of government have been hijacked into the service of special interests. We must redirect government to serve the American people.

The absence of accountability is endemic, of long standing. At this point, presidents—our government's chief executives—routinely speak as if they are mere spectators to their own administrations. If one seeks answers to basic questions about the operations of government, one encounters a fog of euphemisms and evasions. Charles Dickens captured this tendency in nineteenth-century Britain. He memorably wrote of that infinite redirect loop, "the circumlocution office."

Politicians—from presidents on down—are entirely comfortable speaking about *inputs.* By contrast, they evade accountability for *outputs.* When we demand real-world results, they recount their votes for public spending. Budgets are a necessary metric in evaluating programmatic performance—but they are far from sufficient.

In Washington, when a law is passed, politicians crow about the accomplishment. They presume that if they enact a statute or a regulation, the essential work is done. In fact, as citizens know, the real work has only just begun. Laws create a wireframe for action; their passage does not mean the action is done.

The confusion of inputs and outputs is reinforced by the fact that so many of our elected and appointed officials are lawyers. As such, they are especially susceptible to confusing words with deeds, process with substance.

The problem runs deeper, however. The drafting and passage and enactment and implementation and enforcement of laws is increasingly determined by special interests. *Outputs* sought by special interests tend to be *inputs* in the political process.

Special interests regard a law to be a success if it creates value for them. Public officials, annexed to the Special Interest State, all too often accept the special interests' definition of success. By contrast, the outputs sought by the public are relegated to rhetoric.

Several steps can be undertaken immediately to impose accountability on our federal government:

Convene a twenty-first-century Hoover Commission on government reorganization. In the mid-twentieth century, President Truman asked former president Hoover to lead a review of executive branch organization. Truman recognized the need to evaluate and rationalize the extraordinary expansion of bureaucracy created in response to the Great Depression and the Second World War. The Hoover Commission recommended a series of changes. They were implemented over a number of years, completed in the succeeding Eisenhower administration.

At the dawn of the twenty-first century, thoroughgoing executive-branch reorganization is overdue.

Entire areas of government are out of date, duplicative, and unaccountable for the results they were established to achieve. For example, the Environmental Protection Agency, the Department of Energy, the Food and Drug Administration, the National Oceans and Atmospheric Administration, and the Department of Commerce are enmeshed in a welter of interlaced bureaucracy.

Organizational dysfunction can be lethal. In 2015, former secretary of state Colin Powell admitted: "If we had known the intelligence was wrong, we would not have gone into Iraq. But the intelligence community, all 16 agencies, assured us that it was right." One wonders how many more errors and injustices remain unexamined or unaddressed within the darker reaches of the National Security State.

The General Accountability Office produces annual reports on "Additional Opportunities to Reduce Fragmentation, Overlap, and Duplication and Achieve Other Financial Benefits." The dysfunction is so entrenched that it is easy to dismiss it as "old news." The response is so routinized as to amount to its own nascent bureaucracy.

It may all seem hypothetical…until it's not. Citizens seeking to accomplish something concrete from agencies require sophisticated guidance. Navigating the Special Interest State can be a high cost for large companies. It can be implausible or ruinous for individuals and small businesses.

President Obama has noted that the organization of the federal government is rooted in the era of black-and-white television. True enough. The Special Interest State has engendered an invincible entrenchment of the status quo. Congressional committees, closely tied to special interests, resist changes in executive-branch organization that threaten their own privileged positions and relationships.

For this reason, a twenty-first-century Hoover Commission should be charged with reorganization of congressional committees at the same time as federal agencies.

Transparency in the process would ensure that the public has access to information and options. We can all serve as cocreators of a system worthy of its mission. Special interests would be able to take part, but their role would be diminished.

It is important that a new Hoover Commission not be a one-off. The work of reorganization is never done. Serving the public is always a work in progress.

One approach would be to establish a custom that each president reorganizes one sector of government during each four-year term. The specifics could be offered and discussed during presidential campaigns. For example, a candidate committed to action against climate disruption might commit to reorganizing the energy and environment and commerce cluster. Another might seek to rationalize entitlement programs. Yet another might focus on national- or domestic-security agencies.

Consistent with our constitutional framework, this could set the stage for a grand bargain: the executive branch is accorded greater latitude for management and organization; the legislative branch is bolstered in its oversight authority, holding the executive accountable for budgetary and programmatic outputs.

Establish authoritative, uniform standards for government accounting. The national government operates on an annual budget that is nearing $4 trillion. Unfunded liabilities, notably Medicare and Social Security, are also staggering, perhaps over $100 trillion by some estimates. The annual net costs of federal regulations are reckoned, by various experts, in trillions.

The federal government does not have uniform, state-of-the-art cost accounting and capital budgeting. This has numerous negative consequences: absence of managerial controls; diminished congressional oversight; lack of organizational learning; immense waste of resources; and innumerable opportunities for special-interest intervention.

At first glance, these challenges may seem hypothetical or academic. Nonetheless, in a time of constrained resources, when the portion of the national budget that is "discretionary" is being crowded out in favor of politically untouchable items, accounting should become a top priority.

There are numerous ways to accomplish this.

One approach would be to bring in many of the top minds from the activist investor community on Wall Street. They have highly honed capacities to interpret balance sheets. They are attuned to statistical legerdemain. The best are schooled in identifying and unlocking value that others overlook. Such skills could be put to good use, establishing credible, uniform federal government accounting standards. In today's connected world, they could also access the best practices of other nations, as well as those of various states and localities.

There is no reason that the president and the Congress could not undertake these vital reforms immediately.

Mandate annual outputs accountability review for federal government. Given the reach of government and the resources consumed, actionable accountability is needed more than ever. A return to basics is in order.

A strong start could be annual and quarterly reports to the American people from the president and Congress. It is important that they undertake this together at each step.

The two branches should be tasked with agreeing to a discrete series of accountability points for the federal government as whole.

The number might be, for example, ten. One target might be budgetary, such as deficit reduction. Another might be reduction in numbers of homeless people. Another might be meeting specific performance standards for education. Yet another might be defined progress in war or refugee resettlement.

Simplicity is a key. It will require public engagement at each step. The determination of targets, the review of their accomplishment, and the changes made for ongoing improvement should be transparent. The public should not merely be informed, but have opportunities to participate, collaborate, and cocreate.

Mandate annual outputs accountability review for cabinet agencies. In sync with the overall government accountability review, each of the cabinet agencies should be directed to come up with a small number of specific annual outputs. The number might be five, or ten. They would be negotiated between the president and the Congress, with input from the public. They might include the independent inspectors general, who constitute a vastly underutilized resource for monitoring and evaluating government performance.

Mandate presidential-congressional quarterly and annual public discussions. The public could be well served by quarterly, televised discussions between the president and congressional leaders on the progress toward meeting their agreed outputs. They could be moderated and structured by joint agreement. Importantly, they could include questions submitted by citizens in advance, as well as via social media during the presentation.

Mandate annual public discussion including president, chief justice of the United States, and congressional leaders. There is widespread misunderstanding of the role of the Supreme Court. The press and general public often discuss judicial cases as if the high court were a priestly legislature. In the Special Interest State, this is exacerbated by the division of the court along partisan lines, reflecting the philosophical orientation of the presidents who appointed the various members.

Consistent with the separation of powers, it would be enlightening to have the chief justice, the president, and congressional leaders engage in an annual, televised discussion on judicial decisions and directions. These could include questions from the public, both in advance and submitted via social media during the program.

Enforce accountability through salary withholding. We have become inured to repeated failures of the president and Congress to meet budgetary and other constitutional obligations. Whatever shame they might feel is overridden by the complacency of their special-interest sponsors who benefit from the status quo.

One readily achievable means of enforcing accountability is to withhold the salaries of the president (and her appointees) and members of Congress when they fail to achieve a specified task. This might include the appropriations bills for the various parts of the federal government (which are rarely enacted timely); annual budget resolutions; war powers decisions; and other specified, significant outputs.

This could be accomplished by the voluntary, public agreement of the president and Congress. It could be linked to the output commitments proposed above.

This would bring a degree of accountability to government that is normal practice for the rest of us: produce or pay the price.

Some might object that it is overbroad. That is, the failure might be more the fault of the president or the Congress in any given situation; is it fair that they all are penalized? The answer, of course, is that the failure—or the accomplishment—is shared. It's up to them to sort it out.

Impose mandatory sunset of federal statutes, regulations, and programs. In the Special Interest State, government programs, once established, are accepted as permanent. Without clear criteria for success, their work is never done. The "war on drugs," the "war on poverty," the "war on cancer"...These wars are never "won." Our actual wars are no longer defined or "won," either.

A wise approach would be to mandate that all laws, regulations, and programs be "sunsetted," expiring at specific intervals, such as every five years. Thereafter, they would need to be reevaluated and reauthorized by Congress and signed by the president.

Whether sunsetting laws is effective depends upon the commitment of the president and Congress. If the process is transparent, the public can observe and participate and hold officials to account. If the federal government has been reformed along the lines suggested here, sunset provisions could have real teeth.

Perhaps most important over time, the process of review can shift the burden of proof to those who would maintain the status quo. Accountability holds the prospect of changing the culture in Washington. It can expose the special-interest coalitions that accrete laws and programs, all too often rendering them politically untouchable. A rigorous, reliable sunset approach can also set the stage for related reforms, such as zero-based budgeting in the agencies.

Reform civil service laws. The federal civil service system represents some of the best thinking in public administration—from the 1880s. It is an industrial-age construct. Today's public agencies are structured along the lines of large corporations in the twentieth century.

The civil service system has long been impervious to thoroughgoing reform. Public employee unions have an intense motivation to maintain the status quo. Other affected interests may also resist change. Fundamentally, there is a lack of consensus as to the purposes of the federal workforce. Is it to serve the citizens at large? Is it to provide employment for veterans and other meritorious individuals?

In the early twenty-first century, the corporate counterparts to federal agencies are undergoing transformation. The notion of having a career in one industry over the course of one's life, with reliable increases in salary and benefits, has largely disappeared. The civil service is an ever more isolated outlier.

It took exceptional leadership from the likes of Theodore Roosevelt to establish the modern civil service system. It will take at least that to achieve corresponding reform against the massed inertia of the Special Interest State.

A twenty-first-century civil service system should ensure that government has access to the extraordinary human resources arrayed in twenty-first-century America. One test might well be this: Do we make it possible to access the value creation capacities of our most productive and creative people?

In the Special Interest State, it has become all the more difficult to put extraordinary individuals to use. Such talent, unleashed and accountable solely to the public, would be a mortal threat to many indefensible arrangements.

Politics and government should have direct access to individuals and enterprises and networks that are effectively disrupting other areas of our lives and work. If, for example, we cannot come up with ways to effectively engage individuals such as Warren Buffett, Bill Gates, Carl Icahn, Elon Musk, Mark Zuckerberg, and Sheryl Sandberg in our current system, we know we must make changes.

When the website healthcare.gov fails, we need to figure out why the American government is unable to make use of the world's greatest minds in the digital space.

We need to unleash the disruptive dynamism of the American people into our tired governance.

As in other areas, there is a sensible reset in our midst. Congress could grant greater latitude for executive branch management, in exchange for increased accountability for performance metrics.

The arcane area of civil service law and regulation can be forbidding. In the best of circumstances, many people have a bias against human resources as "soft." In fact, opening public tasks to our best talent could unleash untold benefits. Combined with other reforms, it could expose many outdated Special Interest State arrangements to the bracing challenge of new energy, new ideas, and new approaches.

Reform sovereign immunity laws. Recent years have seen a plethora of spectacular failures by government agencies.

Notable instances include:

- the troubled response to Hurricane Katrina by the Federal Emergency Management Agency and others;
- the discharge of millions of gallons of toxic materials into Colorado's Animas River by the Environmental Protection Agency;
- the breach of security of millions of Americans' confidential information by the Office of Personnel Management;
- the exposure of the citizens of Flint, Michigan, to toxic levels of lead in their drinking water over the course of nearly two years—abandoned by local, state, and national agencies;
- the deaths of hundreds of thousands awaiting care from the Veterans Administration.

The absence of accountability is breathtaking. Had a private entity polluted a water body in the way the EPA did, individuals and organizations would have faced civil and criminal investigations and public opprobrium. Yet, when the government does it, there are no comparable consequences. The bureaucrats issue pro forma mea culpas—and everyone is expected to move on as if nothing exceptional occurred.

The disparity brings to mind a quip from comedian Bill Murray: "So, if we lie to the government, it's a felony. But if they lie to us it's politics."

While presidents can be more or less effective in affixing management accountability for such failures, there are limits to legal accountability. Under the longstanding legal doctrine of sovereign immunity, redress against government officials is severely circumscribed. Affected citizens are less protected solely as a result of who is liable for the harm.

The results can be perverse. Generally, because government agencies are protected under sovereign immunity, they are not confronted with the remorseless fate that awaits private entities in similar circumstances. Were the government's reach more limited, this might be less of a concern. In the Special Interest State, as public agencies undertake more and more tasks, this becomes a serious matter.

Properly reformed, sovereign immunity laws can protect government as it undertakes necessary roles. They can incent government to meet the highest standards. They can also prompt consideration of alternatives in the private and not-for-profit sector to best achieve public needs.

Reform conflict-of-interest laws. Conflict-of-interest rules address a foundational question of representative government: Are public officials serving the public—or are they serving special interests?

In the twentieth century, conflict-of-interest rules were established to push back against the tendency of government agencies to be "captured" by the interests they regulate. The focus was on direct financial conflicts of interest. For example, if someone is an investor in a coal company, he should be recused from decisions relating to regulation of the coal industry.

Amid the expansion of the Special Interest State, such a limited conflict-of-interest code is quaint. There are additional areas of conflict and appearance of conflict that should be incorporated:

- Recent, high-profile presidential appointees have received severance bonuses from regulated entities, including health care companies and Wall Street investment firms. Such financial transactions should be included within conflict of interest guidelines. At the very least, there is an appearance of a conflict. It is a legitimate question whether individuals should be confirmed by the Senate to serve in high executive branch positions under such a dark cloud. Actionable transparency can elicit citizen input into their public vetting and evaluation.

- Executive-branch appointees should be subject to an airtight ban on outside business and employment relationships.

  Secondary work relationships pose several problems. They detract from the full-time commitments of executive-branch employees (and the 24/7 expectations of presidential appointees). They are a gateway to divided allegiances and corruption. The business value of federal officials would certainly be greatest where there is an ethically dubious connection between their public and private roles.

- Nonpecuniary conflicts of interest should be included within revised guidelines. In the Special Interest State, additional areas of conflict have arisen.

  An example can be found in environmental regulation. Individuals who are tied to special interests outside of industry are exempted from recusal requirements. This is the case even though officials may previously have been employed by an organization that is participating in a regulatory proceeding.

  Consider the Environmental Protection Agency. As we have noted, the Republicans often appoint officials who come from industry (who are subject to conflict-of-interest rules). The Democrats often appoint officials who come from environmental advocacy groups (who are exempted from the full force of conflict-of-interest rules).

  Those who hail from advocacy organizations may sincerely believe that they represent the "public interest." As such, they might well fail to recognize the conflict of interest.

That is not credible, however. Vis-à-vis the public, all such organizations are special interests. The government must take all of the various positions into account in reaching a disinterested conclusion.

In addition, "public interest" advocacy groups may have financial interests of their own. They may hold government contracts or receive grants. They may be in alliance with regulated corporations or receive funding from them. They may lobby Congress arm-in-arm with the EPA supporting or opposing specific regulations or laws. They may even lobby Congress for or against EPA budget items.

Corresponding issues can arise in the cases of individuals who move into government from foundations or think tanks.

Such situations present real and perceived conflicts of interest. The rules should be updated and extended to encompass the new realities of the Special Interest State.

Restore the Rule of Law

Disrupt Politics

We have now sunk to a depth at which
the restatement of the obvious is the first
duty of intelligent men and women.

—George Orwell

The rule of law is under fire in the United States. People want the laws upheld—until they are adversely affected. In the Special Interest State, laws and regulations are the coin of the realm. They represent centralized direction and control. Each element of the legal process has become subject to special-interest influence.

There are fundamental challenges for reform. One is the tendency to simply pile on new legal requirements without reforming the whole. The resulting complexity can occasion additional problems, both foreseeable and unintended.

There are several steps that can be taken immediately to restore the rule of law:

Restore congressional budget authority. By any yardstick, Congress has abandoned its fundamental, constitutional duty of holding the power of the purse. Rarely is a timely budget achieved. The result is reliance on "continuing resolutions" that extend existing budget items.

By any objective measure, the budget process that Congress established in 1974 is broken. The Special Interest State is, however, well served. There is a strong bias toward the status quo.

Continuing resolutions ratify existing arrangements. They short-circuit the legislative process. The tangled skein of competing congressional committees makes oversight all but impossible. Special-interest influence can flourish, obscured amid the fog of partisan warfare. Vast areas of spending are not methodically reviewed.

A recent, concerning trend is congressional acquiescence in self-financing of agencies via fees, fines, and penalties. This constitutes a complete abdication of constitutional responsibilities. It opens up new areas for special-interest infiltration and abuse.

Reform of the budget process can be achieved in tandem with the reorganization of the legislative and executive branches through a new Hoover Commission. The goals should include simplicity, transparency, timeliness, and comprehensive inclusion of all federal budget items.

Restore congressional war powers. One of the fundamental concerns of the American founders was to ensure that the decision to go to war not be left to an individual. The new office of president was distinguished from monarchy in this critical respect.

It was understood that the executive would require latitude to act in response to crisis. Until the twentieth century, the members of the House and Senate were not in Washington most of the year. Assembling them rapidly in a horse-and-buggy era was no small thing.

Congressional war powers have been eroded beyond recognition. Our nation has not formally declared war since the Second World War. The Korean War, the Vietnam War, the "War on Terror" (including the second Iraq War) were undertaken with constitutional workarounds that yielded immense power to the president.

Note that these were not short-term "police actions" by any reasonable definition. The Korean War cost thirty-four thousand American lives. The Vietnam War cost fifty-eight thousand American lives. Operation Enduring Freedom, in response to the 9/11 attacks, has become the longest war in our history.

Is it a coincidence that the decline in congressional war powers has moved in sync with the decline in the nation's effectiveness on the battlefield? Would the United States have entered and executed these operations with greater clarity of purpose had the nation been engaged in a preliminary debate, followed by a vote of Congress?

Justice Robert H. Jackson, a legal giant of the twentieth century, illuminated the stakes:

> Nothing in our Constitution is plainer than that declaration of a war is entrusted only to Congress. Of course, a state of war may in fact exist without a formal declaration. But no doctrine that the Court could promulgate would seem to me more sinister and alarming than that a President whose conduct of foreign affairs is so largely uncontrolled, and often even is unknown, can vastly enlarge his mastery over the internal affairs of the country by his own commitment of the Nation's armed forces to some foreign venture.

Some object that the constitutional requirement of a declaration of war is outdated. Declaring war against another nation-state, such as Nazi Germany and imperial Japan, conforms to the logic of the Constitution. What about proxy wars, where great nations fight one another indirectly through support for third parties? What about the "War on Terror," with its murderer's row of non-national actors?

One might respond that the constitutional requirement of a declaration of war is even more important in our current circumstances. The national debate could give rise to clarity of purpose and suitability of means. If the president and Congress are unable to come together to define war aims and outcomes concisely, perhaps the entire enterprise merits reconsideration.

In the twenty-first century, there are additional reasons for reviving congressional authority. In our connected world, citizens can engage much more deeply than in the past. The most grievous decisions faced by our elected officials can be illuminated by the insights of our people. The unique American assets of innovation and creativity can be mobilized as never before in our digital age. Through disciplined definition of aims and oversight of means, it is also possible that areas of foreseeable abuse, such as secret operations and tribunals, can be effectively supervised.

Most important, wars undertaken with public and congressional input are more likely to be undertaken with wisdom, implemented with broad citizen participation. The sacrifices should not be disproportionately borne by 1 percent of the population.

For now, the trends continue in the other direction. The George W. Bush and Barack Obama administrations relied on ever more strained claims of authorizations for war making. The resulting morass of legality has effaced accountability beyond recognition.

Recent presidents justify their failure to follow constitutional norms by citing, among other things, the dysfunction of Congress. That is far from persuasive. The challenges of politicians pale in comparison with the travails of our citizens engaged in combat. This rather apparent if unsettling truth is illuminated by the conspicuous absence of military service by recent presidents, executive-branch appointees, members of Congress, and their families. Our politicians are content to take us into war using other people's money and placing other people's fathers and mothers, sons and daughters in harm's way.

A corresponding decline of effective congressional participation is seen in other areas of foreign policy. By any objective understanding, the 2015 agreements relating to Iran's nuclear program should have been submitted to Congress as treaties. As such, they would have been constitutionally required to run the gauntlet of obtaining a two-thirds Senate vote. The arguments to the contrary were so convoluted that only a lawyer could comprehend them.

Instead, the president and Congress settled upon a process that required, in effect, votes of approval from only one-third of the Senate.

This not only limited the legitimacy of the resulting agreement, it also lent itself to a regrettable partisan divide. Most important, the voices of the people were neither heard nor heeded.

The failure to follow the constitutional framework has encouraged a rising reliance on secret side agreements. From the Iran nuclear deal to recent trade pacts, the executive branch has committed to conditions that may be entirely at variance with public understanding or American traditions. They create no-accountability zones where special interests wield privileges that would be hard to justify in the light of day.

These problems can all be addressed without constitutional amendment. One need merely have presidential and congressional candidates commit publicly to complying with them. Enforcement can be at the ballot box.

Simplify statutes. If patriotism is the last refuge of the scoundrel, complexity is the reliable refuge of special interests. At every step, from drafting through implementation through law enforcement, special-interest groups benefit from manipulating the details of statutes and regulations.

There are so many laws enacted by Congress and the president that there is good-faith uncertainty as to what is in the crammed tool box known officially as the US Code. The complexity is such that members of Congress cannot comprehend the details of most of the legislation on which they vote.

Statutes of wide application, with extensive civil and criminal penalties, can defy common understanding, even common sense. One is reminded of James Madison's prescient warning: "It will be of little avail to the people…if the laws be so voluminous that they cannot be read, or so incoherent they cannot be understood."

Consider this core liability provision of the hazardous waste cleanup law known as "Superfund":

> (b) There shall be no liability under subsection (a) of this section for a person otherwise liable who can establish by a preponderance of the evidence that the release or threat of release of a hazardous substance and the damages resulting therefrom were caused solely by—(1) an act of God; (2) an act of war; (3) an act or omission of a third party other than an employee or agent of the defendant, or than one whose act or omission occurs in connection with a contractual relationship, existing directly or indirectly, with the defendant (except where the sole contractual arrangement arises from a published tariff and acceptance for carriage by a common carrier by rail), if the defendant establishes by a preponderance of the evidence that (a) he exercised due care with respect to the hazardous substance concerned, taking into consideration the characteristics of such hazardous substance, in light of all relevant facts and circumstances, and (b) he took precautions against foreseeable acts or omissions of any such third party and the consequences that could foreseeably result from such acts or omissions; or (4) any combination of the foregoing paragraphs.

If Helen of Troy possessed the face that launched a thousand ships, Superfund is a statute that launched a thousand lawsuits. Ironically, at the time of passage, the law was intended to be "temporary."

Ever longer statutes—and the litigation and regulation that ensue—are integral to the operating system of the Special Interest State. Recent legislation—the Affordable Care Act, the Dodd-Frank financial reform—is all but incomprehensible to intelligent people of goodwill. No one could credibly argue that the totality of these laws is optimal. Nevertheless, each line, each word, belongs to someone, somewhere; just tug and you will soon find out where the roots reach.

The *Onion* satirized the public debate ensuing after the enactment of the Affordable Care Act: "Man Who Understands 8% of Obamacare Vigorously Defends It from Man Who Understands 5%." More elegantly, Chief Justice Roberts charitably noted that "the traditional legislative process" was not in evidence. As a result, Roberts continued, "The Act does not reflect the type of care and deliberation that one might expect from such significant legislation."

Behind the apt satire is a troubling reality: the convoluted statutes of recent years are not drafted so that we can comprehend them. In the Special Interest State, they are crafted by and for interest groups and their enabling intermediaries.

Let that sink in: *the laws that bind us are not written so that We the People can comprehend them.* The Special Interest State has resulted in lawmaking focused on serving the powerful and connected—including lawmakers themselves. Quite simply: We the People are not being served.

This represents a fundamental challenge to our constitutional framework. The Congress cannot hold the executive accountable. The public cannot hold anyone accountable. To interpret and comply can be all but impossible for anyone other than the largest, most politically potent corporations and nongovernmental organizations. Enforcement becomes unpredictable—even when not subject to overt political intervention.

The bureaucracies of government and large companies can intersect and derive mutual benefit from such detailed statutes and regulations. Lawyers and other experts also profit, as they navigate the legal and regulatory minefield. They can seek favorable venues for their causes in executive agencies and congressional committees.

In 2015, the New York law firm Davis Polk released a five-year review of the implementation of the Dodd-Frank law. Their snapshot is evocative of the Special Interest State in action:

- 22,296 pages of rule releases published in Federal Register
- 631 regulatory releases by the Commodity Futures Trading Commission, Securities and Exchange Commission, Federal Reserve, Office of the Comptroller of the Currency, and Consumer Financial Protection Bureau
- 139 bills introduced in Congress to amend or repeal the statute

All this to interpret and implement an act whose length defends it against the risk of being read. Anyone care to guess how many members of Congress read and studied it prior to voting it through? Were they relying on the president, who graduated Harvard Law School, to do so?

By contrast, the Glass-Steagall Act that safeguarded American finance capitalism from the 1930s through the 1990s clocked in at a mere thirty thousand words.

Is there any reason that all statutes, henceforth, could not be limited to thirty thousand or fewer words? Any such number is ultimately arbitrary. Still, the principle is sound.

Behold the American tax system. It abounds with special-interest carve-outs and privileges. It poses two kinds of resistance to reform. The first is the inertia that accrues to all regulatory regimes in the Special Interest State. Now, there's a second barrier. ProPublica reports that the leading provider of tax return software lobbies against tax simplification. Would it be surprising if the IRS were to join them, advocating for the status quo?

Gather it all together, and one must agree with the view expressed by the US register of copyrights, reviewing the legal tangle of her subject area: "If one needs an army of lawyers to understand the basic precepts of the law, then it is time for a new law."

The same could be said for almost any area of American law.

Legal reformer Philip Howard persuasively proposes that the United States undertake comprehensive recodification. According to Howard:

> The way this works is that small committees are charged with coming up with simplified codes in each area of government, and then lawmakers decide whether to adopt them. This is how the Justinian and Napoleonic codes were created—it took only five months for Jean-Etienne Portalis and a small committee to propose a complete overhaul of French law. That is also how America's Uniform Commercial Code was created.

Recodification, focused on simplicity and accountability, could, in Howard's words, "unleash enormous productive activity—like replacing a muddy road with a paved highway."

The process of reform, transparently undertaken, could clear away countless special-interest provisions that clog and corrupt our political and legal systems. It is an essential component of restoring constitutional government. Seen in this way, it is clear that the project of legal simplification is far more than a mere paper chase among attorneys. It is central to dismantling the Special Interest State, returning power to the people.

Simplify regulation: Strict standards, rationalized process. Statutes are translated into actions via implementing regulations. Most individuals and enterprises encounter government power through the regulatory process.

In theory, regulations should be clear enough for anyone to comprehend and comply with them. They should be flexible enough to encourage innovation. Moreover, they should impose as few costs as possible, so that scarce resources can be directed to the most valuable purposes.

In practice, our regulatory process falls far short of these criteria. There are various reasons for this regrettable state of affairs.

First, as Ronald Reagan often underscored, powerful interest groups often have outsized influence in the regulatory process. The bureaucracies of large corporations interact with government bureaucracies to create highly prescriptive, bureaucratic rules in their own image. This may or may not be motivated by self-interest, but the consequences are deleterious.

Second, by design or default, highly prescriptive regulations advantage incumbent enterprises. They constitute a very real barrier to entry to new entrants. The penalty is greater for the most innovative, disruptive challengers to the status quo.

Third, politically connected enterprises may persuade government agencies to promulgate regulatory requirements that can only be met by…themselves. For example, criteria for approved technologies may be tightly crafted with specific products or services in mind.

Fourth, regulations may include various avenues for agency or regulatory intervention, review, or appeal. These may be well intended, conceived with an eye toward public comment and inclusion. Whatever the intent, they can wreak uncertainty, inordinate expense, and untold opportunities for mischief making. Special interests benefiting from the status quo are best served. They can extract concessions of various kinds. They can ensure that the costs and risks of change are highlighted among concerned parties, while the prospective benefits are inevitably, comparatively uncertain.

Reimagining regulation should begin with a relentless adherence to principles of simplicity, ease of compliance, and clarity of enforcement. There should be provisions for actionable transparency and accountability at every step. Regulations, including in the most technical areas, should set *high standards or goals*, achieved through *simplified, streamlined, efficient procedures.*

This would represent a transformative change from our current circumstances. Today, standards are often low or muddled, and process is convoluted. Smart reform would advance the public interest. It would invite citizen participation throughout, supercharged through Internet and social media tools.

Combined with simplified statutes, simplified regulations would help strip the gears of the Special Interest State.

Require single-purpose legislation. One of the most unwelcome, recurring news stories from Washington is that congressional action on major legislation is stopped in its tracks amid controversy over an unrelated item. Individuals or small groups of members may seek negotiating leverage, amending widely supported bills with unrelated provisions.

A characteristic example was the delay in passage of a widely supported human trafficking bill to deal with an extraneous provision relating to abortion funding. At least one major presidential appointment, subject to Senate confirmation, was caught up in the same delay.

Such legislative chicanery can impose delays that have real-world consequences. It empowers a minority of the Senate to thwart the will of the majority. This is accentuated today, when the legacy parties are ever more polarized, with fewer members amenable to thoughtful compromise. Perhaps most importantly, the legislation that results will have eluded the full vetting of the legislative process, much less public review and opportunity to participate from the outside.

The Congress should commit to limiting each piece of legislation to a single purpose. That will not end all arguments about what constitutes a single purpose. Nonetheless, it could establish a standard by which bills would be evaluated.

Restore a strict law-enforcement ethos. Just as special interests have hijacked legislative authority in the making of laws, they have seized executive authority in the enforcement of laws. When enforcement is broken, other aspects of the legal system are also damaged.

The first obligation of the president is to enforce the law. The oath of office states:

> I do solemnly swear (or affirm) that I will faithfully execute the office of President of the United States, and will to the best of my ability, preserve, protect, and defend the Constitution of the United States.

The Constitution, Article II, Section 3, requires that the president "shall take Care that the Laws be faithfully executed."

In the Special Interest State, even this foundational obligation is suborned. Statutory authorities lie unused when they are politically unpalatable. For example, no recent president has vigorously applied the enforcement authorities relating to illegal immigration. The president who pushed Obamacare unilaterally suspended enforcement of a series of statutory milestones. While contending advocates quarrel for decades about gun-control laws, key elements of existing law remain unenforced. The examples are escalating, in number and seriousness, with no end in sight.

So, too, there is risk from the power of law enforcement being brought to bear against politically disfavored individuals and groups. In 1940, Robert Jackson, serving as attorney general, counseled prudence to the assembled US attorneys:

> The prosecutor has more control over life, liberty and reputation than any other person in America. His discretion is tremendous…Therein is the most dangerous power of the

> prosecutor: that he will pick people that he thinks he should get, rather than pick cases that need to be prosecuted. With the law books filled with a great assortment of crimes, a prosecutor stands a fair chance of finding at least a technical violation of some act on the part of almost anyone.

The election of one or other of the legacy parties to the presidency is intended to reorient national priorities. It is not a blank check to skirt constitutional safeguards. It is not an authorization to bypass the legislative branch and statutory mandates in accord with passing popular enthusiasms or the tides of political power.

The evolution of the Special Interest State poses another challenge. The executive branch, including nominally "independent" agencies, is entrusted with interpreting and implementing the laws. Regulatory agencies' interpretations of their legal authorities are accorded great deference by the courts. The result is the rise of an increasingly unaccountable administrative arm of the Special Interest State.

The stakes are high. The Justice Department, reviewing the issue, has summarized the Supreme Court's constitutional interpretation: "The Executive cannot, under the guise of exercising enforcement discretion, attempt to effectively rewrite the laws to match its policy preferences."

Strict, impartial law enforcement is critical to effective governance:

- It creates an incentive for legal simplicity. It can be difficult to enforce laws that are overly complex. Given that such laws are also difficult to comprehend and comply with, this is a useful feedback mechanism.
- It heightens pressure on elective officials to reform laws that are not in sync with public attitudes.

- It prompts legislators to take drafting seriously. When law enforcement is spotty and politicized, they may feel less pressure to get it right from the start.
- It constitutes a counterbalance against the tendency to pass too many laws. In recent years the numbers of federal crimes have soared. Much of this is to score political points in the short term. The problems arise further down the line. Risks of injustice and prosecutorial abuse are heightened.

Restoring strict law enforcement will not happen overnight. Raising awareness and holding the president and Congress accountable at the ballot box can be a strong start.

Slash Government Overhead

America was created in defiance of government power asserted across the sea and around the world, from London. Independence binds our national DNA.

The subsequent centralization of power in Washington, DC, began, in large part, in reaction to the centralization of power in finance and industry in the late nineteenth and early twentieth centuries. The push and pull of federalism has always been with us.

As the Special Interest State has evolved, the persistent resistance to change has frozen outdated arrangements into place. All too often, citizens, as well as state and local governments, must travel great distances, hat in hand, to Washington, DC. They seek resolution of matters close to home. By contrast, special interests are nestled in the nation's capital.

Since the mid-twentieth century, there has been a widespread presumption that almost any issue can be resolved through national political action. If you wish to impose your view on others, there is a great temptation to seek a federal law. Inevitably, various components of the Special Interest State are brought into the drafting, enactment, implementation and enforcement of new statutes and regulations.

The Special Interest State retains a top-down, one-size-fits-all mind-set. Each of the legacy parties indulges in a fitful federalism. On the issues that matter most to their special-interest sponsors, they have no hesitation in tamping down state and local autonomy.

The legacy-party proclivity to centralized direction sits uncomfortably if not precariously in the twenty-first century. From the European Union to the People's Republic of China, there is rising restiveness. The privileges of elites are under scrutiny. There is a discomfiting disconnect between the words of those who make the laws and the realities of those who experience them.

The Special Interest State has wrought rampant dysfunction. "Made in Washington, DC" has become a warning label.

An example is infrastructure. This is an area with a recognized federal government role and responsibility. Its history includes major accomplishments, from the era of "internal improvements" to the establishment of the interstate highway system. Today, Americans are acutely aware that our infrastructure is in disrepair—to the point of pockmarked roads and highways and collapsing bridges. Compared to our international competitors, we are glaringly out of date, living off the value created by past generations.

The Special Interest State has proven startlingly inept in addressing our infrastructure deficits. Common Good, led by Philip Howard, reports: "Delays in approving infrastructure projects cost the nation more than twice what it would cost to fix the infrastructure." The numbers create a stark picture: delays in public projects have cost the nation more than $3.7 trillion. By contrast, the price of modernizing infrastructure is pegged at $1.7 trillion.

Common Good provided an after-action analysis of the 2009 economic stimulus, which was intended to jump-start infrastructure modernization. They highlight a White House five-year update on the stimulus: "A grand total of $30 billion (3.6 percent of the stimulus) had been spent on transportation infrastructure."

Such numbers can surely be disputed at the margins. The essential point is indisputable: the overhead for federal government action has become far too significant to ignore.

In sync with the decentralizing tendencies of the information age, institutions closer to the people have gained strength. State and local governments, the private sector, not-for-profit organizations, and ad hoc networks assume ever-greater roles. This is seen even in matters that are international in scope, such as responding to the risks of climate disruption. Citizens—and cities—are the engines of real-time changes, while Washington remains enmeshed in a morass of rhetoric.

In response to these rising realities, a first step would be to systematically quantify the costs and trade-offs associated with government actions at various levels, through various means.

Mandate overhead impact statements. Environmental impact statements were created as a policy innovation in the late 1960s and early 1970s. They are intended to ensure that environmental consequences are taken into account in government decision making. The EIS process includes two key elements: first, the environmental risks or results are identified; second, a series of options is crafted. The EIS process not only affects specific policies and project determinations; it also influences the broader culture from which policies emerge.

The EIS process has been justly criticized for its implementation. Nonetheless, the concept could have value, updated and applied to quantify overhead and mandate the presentation of alternatives.

Proposed budget and programmatic items could be analyzed for the overhead required for their implementation. Each level of government—federal, state, local—could be included. So, too, options in the private and not-for-profit sectors would enable legislators, the president, and the public to weigh the costs and benefits of various approaches. There is also every reason, in the information age, to look to the experiences of other nations for ideas. Most important, input can also be sought from citizens in a transparent process.

Overhead impact statements could aggregate now scattered data on program performance. Issues such as permitting and litigation could be taken into account. Duplicative government agency actions could be isolated.

They could also focus attention on fundamental questions that are, all too often, elided today. What are the cost differentials in consolidating grant and welfare programs? How many resources could be redeployed if beneficiaries were to receive cash rather than in-kind benefits?

Can administrative costs of health insurance, including private policies, be reduced and reallocated toward patients' needs? Credible studies indicate that fraud consumes as much as five percent of American health-care spending.

The US Department of Energy has estimated that as much as one-half of costs of rooftop solar installation are "administrative." How much faster can residential solar options penetrate the market if the relevant permitting and financing mechanisms are rationalized?

Note that there is not an inevitable ideological tilt to quantifying overhead and considering budget and program options. In some cases, a nongovernmental approach might be chosen. In others, such as the overhead in the current health-care system, a strong case might be made for a single-payer alternative. In still others, hybrid approaches might be created from crowd-sourced public participation.

The "one right way" reflexively offered by the legacy parties' dated ideologies of pro- or antigovernment would be put to the test. Accountability would be continual. For government, as for the rest of us, changing circumstances would be met with evolving approaches, driven by data.

Quantification can be transformative. The late senator Daniel Patrick Moynihan spoke eloquently of the significance of developing generally accepted statistical measures of unemployment during the New Deal. Such data became an output measure for government policy—and a publicly understood accountability metric.

In an era when our national resources are strained to meet expectations, every dollar must be safeguarded. The overhead occasioned by special-interest arrangements represents unjustifiable cost that can be redeployed to create value for the public.

For all these reasons, it is essential that overhead impact statements be applied to existing programs as well as new proposals. For example, they could be required as part of the mandatory sunset process of laws and regulations. The prospect of such accountability could also breathe life into dormant congressional oversight in the meantime.

Special interests have spawned a myriad of tollbooths clogging the road to twenty-first-century progress and possibility. It is past time to make them justify their costs—or sweep them away.

Transform through Transparency

The French essayist Paul Valéry observed, "Politics is the art of preventing people from taking part in affairs which properly concern them." By this standard, the Special Interest State is succeeding brilliantly.

Sir Paul McCartney has said, "If slaughterhouses had glass walls, everyone would be vegetarians." If the Special Interest State had glass walls, we would all be reformers.

Transparency can be transformative. It is in our rights to demand it.

All too often today, our public servants collaborate with special interests, in connivance vis-à-vis the citizens. Consider the extraordinary statement of a professor, Jonathan Gruber, publicly taking a victory lap following the enactment of Obamacare:

> Lack of transparency is a huge political advantage. Basically, call it the stupidity of the American voter or whatever, but basically that was really, really critical to getting the thing to pass.

This is what journalist Michael Kinsley calls a gaffe: a person in politics who inadvertently expresses the unadorned truth.

We the People are not stupid. All too often, though, we're not informed. If we yield our power to the Special Interest State, it is on us.

Our constitutional government is based on the consent of the governed. The prerogatives of centralized, top-down organizations are increasingly difficult to defend. In the twenty-first century, information is dispersed. Innovation tends to arise from the bottom up, from the outside in.

It is fair enough to compare today's top officials unfavorably with the nation's founders. It is also true that we possess the means to draw upon the extraordinary energy and wisdom of more than 320 million Americans.

Transparency is an instrumental goal. It enables us to better achieve our fundamental rights and duties of self-government. It is an indispensable link, connecting the people and our government in a living network of collective intelligence. Special interests can add value by participating in that network. They should not, however, ally themselves with the government vis-à-vis the rest of us.

Make enforceable transparency the default for government activity. Recent presidential candidates routinely commit to open the activities of government to public view. President Obama, for example, declared that his would be "the most transparent administration in history."

His administration's abject failure to meet his own standard is matched by corresponding declarations from other recent presidents. One finds similar words scattered on the floor of abandoned congressional promises.

The principles are clear enough. They are well summarized in the memorandum on "Transparency and Open Government" released by the White House on the second day of the first Obama administration, January 21, 2009:

- "Government should be transparent."
- "Government should be participatory." The people should have the capacity to effectively take part in their government. Government's actions should reflect the views and values of those who are to be served.
- "Government should be collaborative." Using information-age tools, government activities should be undertaken as joint ventures with citizens.

Transparency is consistent with the Constitution's vision and structure. It holds the potential for making government serve more effectively from every vantage point. The rising use of data in the business and the not-for-profit sectors has manifest applicability to the processes of crafting and implementing laws and regulations.

There is an implacable obstacle: Transparency is a lethal threat to the existing arrangements of officeholders and their special-interest sponsors.

The result is that government initiatives for transparency are spasmodic. The records and activities of various officials are scrutinized for evidence of the influence of lobbyists. In some cases, this may add value. It is also an invitation to public officials to elude accountability through parallel, personal e-mail and cell phone accounts and the like.

More central is the failure of transparency at key moments in the legislative and regulatory processes. We have noted the passage of the notorious "cromnibus" budget package in December 2014. Within weeks of an electoral earthquake intended to shake up Washington, the lame-duck Congress and the president joined hands, jamming this essential legislation through, chockablock with unexamined provisions.

There was no pretense of transparency. The speed required swept away the patina of deliberation customarily imparted by empty formalities. It might be seen as the Special Interest State unplugged. Had the provisions of the legislation been subjected to the textbook sequence, through committee development, the working products could have been posted online for public review and input. Even if all the issues were exempted from the committee gauntlet, the provisions of the continuing resolution could have been posted online sufficiently in advance for meaningful public participation.

Effective transparency can be achieved by mandating reasonable periods for posting and receiving input on legislative and executive activities. There is no magic to setting the times and circumstances for such opportunities. They simply need to be available in a way that renders them actionable for citizens.

Transparency provisions can be given life by making them enforceable. For example, transparency deadlines and milestones can be codified as mandatory duties of government. Citizens could be accorded the right to ask a court to block noncompliant laws or regulations from taking effect.

The government is also the curator of an immense trove of data. Much of it is, practically speaking, accessible only to experts and the well connected. The value created by these Special Interest State intermediaries is overhead from the point of view of the public. The capacity of entrepreneurs to unlock value from such data is far too limited.

The injunction holds true: "Information is power." Real-time transparency can return more of that power to the public.

Data can be standardized within and among agencies. User interfaces can be simplified and enabled through sophisticated information technology. Private enterprises—from Amazon.com to brokerage houses to Uber to Federal Express to various news aggregators—have shown the way.

What is required is a change of expectation, enforced by elections.

A necessary start is to review, revise, implement, and enforce a twenty-first-century Freedom of Information Act (FOIA). The current version of this vital statute was enacted in 1966.

Unsurprisingly, it's about as outmoded as the computers of fifty years ago. FOIA was intended to actualize "a general philosophy of full agency disclosure." A reset of this law to meet twenty-first-century norms is essential. Simplicity, clarity, enforceability, low cost, and ease of access should be hallmarks. A new FOIA should enable and encourage citizen involvement, in various, evolving forms, in every aspect of government operations.

Such reform should ensure that all instrumentalities of governance are included. For example, government-sponsored entities such as the Federal Home Loan Mortgage Corporation (Freddie Mac) and the Federal National Mortgage Association (Fannie Mae) have been subject to litigation challenging their claims to be outside the strictures of FOIA. The principle should be uniform standards, universally applied.

As important as enhanced citizen participation and crowdsourcing can be, they will never replace the representative roles of the legislative and executive branches. In fact, they can enhance the effectiveness and accountability of public officials.

It is well said that the smartest person in the room is, always…the room. Imagine how much innovation can be unleashed from more than three hundred million Americans at this hinge moment.

Some will object, in good faith, that transparency poses danger: they believe that you and I do not know enough to have useful opinions on any number of matters. To be sure, we might well make mistakes.

Such objections have been raised throughout the history of our American experiment. Speaking on behalf of We the People, Thomas Jefferson responded for his time—and ours:

> I know of no safe depository of the ultimate powers of the society but the people themselves; and if we think them not enlightened enough to exercise their control with a wholesome discretion, the remedy is not to take it from them but to inform their discretion.

Mandate comprehensive campaign-finance transparency. Our campaign-finance system has been distorted by the evolution of the Special Interest State. Currently, there is a trifecta of systemic corruption: massive amounts of dark money spending has obscured the sources of funding; lenient legal requirements for "nonpolitical" fundraising organizations have incented candidates to tacitly or covertly coordinate with unaccountable donor groups; and campaign laws, regulations, and enforcement are hobbled by the inevitable conflict of interest of the politicians who hold the pen.

The results are all around us. In October 2014, in the run-up to the midterm elections, the *New York Times* reported:

> More than half of the general election advertising aired by outside groups in the battle for control of Congress has come from organizations that disclose little or nothing about their donors, a flood of secret money that is now at the center of the debate over the line between free speech and corruption.

As we have seen, the Supreme Court has grappled for forty years with the balance between two key values: protecting First Amendment freedoms of political expression and reducing the appearance and reality of corruption presented by massive campaign spending.

In 1976, in the landmark case *Buckley v. Valeo*, the court tilted toward greater regulation of contributions to avoid corruption:

> Congress was surely entitled to conclude that disclosure was only a partial measure and that contribution ceilings were a necessary legislative concomitant to deal with the reality or appearance of corruption in a system permitting unlimited financial contributions, even when the identities and the amounts of the contributions are fully disclosed.

In 2014, in *McCutcheon v. Federal Election Commission*, the court held that aggregate limits on campaign donations infringed upon First

Amendment free expression. With a nod to the new realities of our information age, Chief Justice Roberts highlighted the heightened power of disclosure:

> With modern technology, disclosure now offers a particularly effective means of arming the voting public with information. In 1976, the Court observed that Congress could regard disclosure as "only a partial measure." That perception was understandable in a world in which information about campaign contributions was filed at FEC offices and was therefore virtually inaccessible to the average member of the public. Today, given the Internet, disclosure offers much more robust protections against corruption. Reports and databases are available on the FEC's website almost immediately after they are filed, supplemented by private entities such as Open-Secrets.org and FollowTheMoney.org. Because massive quantities of information can be accessed at the click of a mouse, disclosure is effective to a degree not possible [when earlier cases were decided]. [legal citations omitted]

The chief justice noted that limits on direct contributions to official campaigns might, in practice, encourage prospective donors to turn to a range of entities for which disclosure is not required.

In this and other opinions, a majority of current justices have suggested that mandatory disclosure of political contributions would pass constitutional muster. The implication is clear: recognition of campaign spending as free expression should be accompanied by strong disclosure requirements.

Ultimately, the lack of trust in our public institutions tips the scale toward enforceable, actionable transparency.

Nonetheless, the Congress and the president—as well as most of the states—have failed to impose a strict disclosure regime. They should take action now. A real-time disclosure regime must reach a high and rising level of transparency. The fundamental goal is to ensure that voters are fully informed, in advance of elections, of the identity of donors and the amount of their contributions.

Immediate Internet reporting of expenditures and fundraising would be essential. It should encompass all manner of entities. Such a law should be brief and unambiguous, with strict liability for violations.

Significant violations of reporting requirements should be subject to consequences that would serve as a deterrent. Such penalties might range from forfeiture of victory in tainted elections to a lifetime bar on subsequent office holding by the candidate. As with other areas prone to special-interest influence and politicians' self-interest, the integrity of the process can be advanced by provisions for citizen review and enforcement.

Thus, corporations and unions should be required to publicly disclose all political activities. Today, only a few public companies disclose political activities to shareholders. Labor union reporting is limited in scope. Disclosure should be made extensive and parallel, enabling all citizens to obtain an accurate understanding, without discouraging levels of complexity or cost.

This can begin immediately, through regulatory action from the Internal Revenue Service, the Securities and Exchange Commission, and other agencies. When combined with greater transparency in the executive and legislative branches, such information could be immensely illuminating.

Requiring transparency of 501(c)(4) "social welfare" organizations would remove the predominant source of dark money flooding elections. This would force companies, unions, and advocacy groups who have cloaked their activities to face the harsh light of public scrutiny for the first time. It would ensure that public officials answer first to the voters, rather than special interests.

As important as this step would be, it is not enough. There is every reason to require that all tax-exempt, 501(c) organizations disclose all contributions and expenditures. Their privileged tax status makes such requirements eminently reasonable.

As the revelations relating to the Clinton Foundation have demonstrated, the absence of transparency in "nonpolitical" 501(c)(3) enterprises has metastasized into a refuge for dubious political, governmental, and interest-group relationships. Ongoing revelations of donations by foreign governments and interests, by companies and unions and not-for-profit organizations, point to the need for radical transparency, independently enforced.

Presently, donations to 501(c)(3) organizations can be an effective avenue for veiled interaction with and access to politically influential individuals and organizations. There may be no immediate quid pro quo. The benefit may come later, through apparently unrelated favors.

Donors may also support foundations to create or maintain favorable relationships with current or prospective officeholders. In the case of the Clinton Foundation, special interests—including foreign governments—may have sought to influence a sitting public official with relevant responsibilities, then secretary of state Hillary Clinton. So, too, the Clinton Foundation provided funding for her to supplement the salaries of government officials and to retain outsiders whom the White House barred her from hiring in an official capacity.

Generally, 501(c) organizations maintain secrecy over donations from individuals and organizations that benefit from the appearance of disinterested advocacy. For example, law firms may contribute, seeking third-party support for legislation or regulation favoring their clients. In some cases, competing companies or affected unions have covertly funded citizen groups that are advancing their commercial interests.

Without comprehensive coverage that includes all 501(c) entities, one can be sure that cunning lawyers will continue to conjure up colorable arguments for evading the harsh illumination of actionable transparency.

State-of-the-art political influence is protean in its adaptability. For example, for influential political figures to be paid millions of dollars in speaking fees, including on behalf of foundations, constitutes activity the public should be able to evaluate. So, too, in recent years, foundations associated with ostensibly transparent entities, such as universities, receive and disburse monies outside public view. As a practical matter, this can constitute an evasion of public accountability for the anchor institution.

Such disclosure requirements would also sweep in nominally nonpolitical organizations such as think tanks. These have grown in influence in recent years. Various interests may donate, with an eye toward obtaining apparently unbiased support for their policy positions. Senator Elizabeth Warren has taken a lead role in exposing such arrangements.

There's no doubt that requiring such disclosure would be resisted by some for self-interested reasons. Others might express sincere concern that free expression could be chilled, particularly for controversial causes. Justice Antonin Scalia responded decisively, "There are laws against threats and intimidation; and harsh criticism, short of unlawful action, is a price our people have traditionally been willing to pay for self-governance."

The Special Interest State extends its dominion in the shadows cast by the twilight of representative government. Transparency can be a remorseless corrective, illuminating more and more areas of concern to citizens.

Actionable transparency can be advanced by the use of twenty-first-century digital tools. Combined with rising public expectations, this can prompt transformative change. It will reach in directions we cannot foresee, toward untold possibilities for creating value and affixing accountability.

Create Twenty-First-Century Constitutional Government

In the midst of disruption across so many aspects of our lives and work, our government and politics are conspicuous citadels of privilege. They remain resistant to innovation and accountability.

The operations of our government institutions are largely based on twentieth-century visions and circumstances. In turn, the twentieth-century visions were based on nineteenth-century innovations and experiences.

In their useful book *The Fourth Revolution*, John Micklethwait and Adrian Wooldridge list "the four terrible assumptions" underlying government's present dysfunction:

- "That [government] organizations should do as much as possible in-house, just as carmakers once smelted their own steel." One practical result is that special interests are annexed into governance.
- "That decision making should be centralized." This was a source of great value creation in the early twentieth century, when government rose in tandem with industrial capitalism. In today's interconnected information age, it is a costly anachronism.
- "That public institutions should be as uniform as possible." Bureaucracy is intended to ensure equal treatment and predictability. Instead, it has become a disordered organism, preyed upon by special interests, protected by untouchable political arrangements.
- "That change is always for the worse." The Special Interest State has set institutional blockage against change. It discourages experimentation. It punishes and expels outliers. Administrators protect themselves by resisting innovation—even when proven effective in comparable circumstances.

Such isolation is extraordinary in our interconnected world. The real-time results can be tragic. The Special Interest State is a closed-loop system that resists aggregation of information and the accountability that naturally follows. One example: Micklethwait and Wooldridge cite data suggesting that the gap in education effectiveness between states costs the United States as much as $700 billion per year, comparable to 5 percent of GNP.

The twentieth-century notions that are failing us were always difficult to reconcile with our Constitution. Fortunately, our twenty-first-century goals can be advanced by greater adherence to constitutional governance.

There is every reason to question the presumptive deference to centralized decision making that prompts us to look to Washington, DC, to solve our problems or enforce our will on one another.

The entire relationship between Washington, DC, and the American people is past due for a reset. In practice as well as rhetoric, our government must serve us. If the status quo were working well, it would still need to adapt to the rapid pace of twenty-first-century change. As it is, not only is our governance dysfunctional—the Special Interest State serves interests other than our own.

Replacing the Special Interest State with a constitutional operating system can bring Washington, DC, into the digital age. It can merge our governance with what might be called the Internet ethos. In the words of Joi Ito of MIT Media Lab, "The Internet isn't really a technology. It's a belief system, a philosophy about the effectiveness of decentralized, bottom-up innovation. And it's a philosophy that has begun to change how we think about creativity itself."

As in other fields, the leadership required for twenty-first-century politics is all about service. Leaders are no longer bosses giving direction from the top or at the center. Instead, they do only the things that others cannot do. That includes casting a unifying vision and persuading others to join. It includes accountability for agreed results. It means empowering others at the levels closest to the action.

Leadership means influence and accountability, not domination and delusions of omniscience.

The first phase of the information age has been a boon to the Special Interest State. Politicians and their special-interest sponsors have used digital tools to advance their goals. Political action—from gerrymandering to various avenues of voter education to tracking the voting records and activities of elected officials—has been brought ever more within their dominion.

We are entering the second phase. Information-age tools are, increasingly, making it possible for citizens located far from Washington, DC, to obtain information and affix accountability.

In the twenty-first century, the ideals of the Declaration of Independence can be achieved through the institutions of the Constitution. The founders made *We the People* the first words, the foundation of all else in our Constitution. *We the People* can now apply twenty-first-century capabilities to have the first and last word in our own governance.

We have the power to recast our federal government as a platform, with varied, ever-evolving applications to serve the American people. When one app works, it might be maintained and improved. When another app disappoints, we can learn from the experiment and apply the experience to create value in other ways.

Moving in this direction amounts to an experiment. It requires that we continually reform our governance with the energy and faith required for a successful startup enterprise. At all costs, we must resist the temptation to give up or to regard American government as an invincible incumbent, resting on its laurels from past glories.

Our nation's founders undertook the ultimate start-up. They had "skin in the game." They might remind us what America has always been: an extraordinary evolving experiment, built on the foundation of a free people, united by shared ideals.

Disrupt Politics

A Twenty-First-Century Declaration of Independence

Theme

The Constitution can serve as a highly effective operating system for twenty-first-century politics and government. Revitalizing the institutions of the Constitution will equip us to fulfill the ideals of the Declaration of Independence.

Elements

Restore constitutional government.

- Bring down the twin pillars of the Special Interest State:
  - End the legacy-party duopoly.
  - Establish twenty-first-century Citizen Congress and presidency.
- Demand accountability.
- Restore rule of law.
- Slash government overhead.
- Transform through transparency.

Create twenty-first-century, constitutional government.

The Boston Massacre by Paul Revere, 1770

Four

Would You Have Signed the Declaration of Independence?

Remember, democracy never lasts long. It soon wastes, exhausts, and murders itself. There never was a democracy yet that did not commit suicide.

—John Adams

Posterity—you will never know how much it has cost my generation to preserve your freedom. I hope you will make good use of it.

—John Quincy Adams

Would *you* have signed the Declaration of Independence?

Before you look up in appalled disbelief that anyone would manifest such egregious effrontery as to ask such a question, reflect on it:

Would you have signed the Declaration of Independence?

Declaration Might Well Have Been a Suicide Note

The words of the declaration are unambiguous. They were addressed directly to the sovereign, King George III:

> We, therefore, the Representatives of the united States of America, in General Congress, Assembled, appealing to the Supreme Judge of the world for the rectitude of our intentions, do, in the Name, and by Authority of the good People of these Colonies, solemnly publish and declare, That these united Colonies are, and of Right ought to be Free and Independent States, that they are Absolved from all Allegiance to the British Crown, and that all political connection between them and the State of Great Britain, is and ought to be totally dissolved; and that as Free and Independent States, they have full Power to levy War, conclude Peace, contract Alliances, establish Commerce, and to do all other Acts and Things which Independent States may of right do. And for the support of this Declaration, with a firm reliance on the protection of Divine Providence, *we mutually pledge to each other our Lives, our Fortunes, and our sacred Honor.* [emphasis added]

With one document, solemnized with their signatures, the signers abjured their national identity, their cultural ancestry, and their rights under the law of the land.

They were not only challenging King George III's rule of the American colonies. Their rationale constituted an incendiary challenge to the legitimacy of the monarchy itself. The result was something more dangerous than conventional treason. It was a revolution of the mind, a revolution without boundaries.

They were going all in.

And they were doing so against the most fearsome military machine in the world.

Many would pay a terrible price.

Table Stakes

In the twentieth century, some critics of the Revolution focused on the undoubted wealth and privilege of many of the founders. It is then suggested, by some, that they were acting in their material self-interest in challenging the crown.

Motivation is not as readily comprehended as results. The fact is, those with the most assets had the most to lose–in a material sense–in a revolution that was far from preordained to succeed. The wiser heads among them recognized that subsequently establishing a government–and a nation–on the principles of the declaration would be an unprecedented experiment. The vast American colonial holdings were far larger than city-states.

If anything, the privileged positions of many of the founders renders their determination to rebel all the more unexpected.

Many Americans were loyalists, maintaining their support of the English crown. Estimates of their numbers vary. There appears to be a consensus that somewhere around 15–20 percent of the colonists were Tories. That may understate the reality.

Those who supported the defeated side in wars tend to downplay their involvement on the wrong side of history. So, too, the Tories included many of the most privileged colonists, so they would have had a disproportionate influence.

What about You?

When you truly examine your own life, do you think you would have decided to be a revolutionary in 1776, putting it all on the line? Or would you have been a loyalist? Might you have watched and waited, seen how things were turning before putting your and your loved ones' life, liberty, and property into the cause?

Would you have been willing to divide your family? Benjamin Franklin and many others did.

When have you been unconventional *in your own context,* gone against the grain, isolated yourself, placed your prospects at risk?

Would your decision be different at various times in your life?

When have you gone *all in*?

What about Now?

Are you prepared to work for a new Declaration of Independence from the Special Interest State?

Would you join efforts to complete far-reaching changes by 2026—the 250th anniversary of the original Declaration of Independence?

Coda

It Always Seems Impossible...

It always seems impossible, until it's done.

—Nelson Mandela

Nelson Mandela casting vote in first free election in South Africa, 27 April 1994

We must not be afraid of dreaming the seemingly impossible if we want the seemingly impossible to become a reality.

—Vaclav Havel

The Fall of the Berlin Wall, 1989

Disrupt Politics

When the architects of our republic wrote the magnificent words of the Constitution and the Declaration of Independence, they were signing a promissory note to which every American was to fall heir. This note was a promise that all men, yes, black men as well as white men, would be guaranteed the unalienable rights of life, liberty, and the pursuit of happiness.

—Martin Luther King, Jr.

March on Washington, 28 August 1963

No republic can last if corruption is allowed to eat into its public life. No republic can last if the private citizens sit supinely by and either encourage or tolerate corruption among their representatives.

—Theodore Roosevelt

Theodore Roosevelt

Acknowledgments

Special thanks are owed to the following, who have contributed insights and information in conversations and correspondence: James Alston, Kare Anderson, Howard Berman, Anoop Bose, Meredith Brenalvirez, Ken Cohen, Stephen Couch, Ted Davenport, Scott Ferguson, Ed Fox, William Frank, Natalie Geary, Michael Golden, Michael Grossman, Susanna Haass, Gail and Reed Hatkoff, Jay Heiler, Hugh Hewitt, Philip K. Howard, Charles Jensen, Derek Leebaert, Matt Lewis, Paul Lippe, Rick McGuire, Rick McNeil, Ken Miller, George Montgomery, Dennis Mullins, Mike Myatt, Wayne Nastri, Beverly and John Passerello, Barbara and Richard Pivnicka, Courtney Price, M.S. Rao, Juergen Resch, Nancy and Scott Robertson, Joe Rodota, Brad Schick, Dan Schnur, Terry Scott, Tom Shiroda, Richard Norton Smith, Stephen Merrill Smith, Nick Sorrentino, Karen Spencer, Michelle Spray, Ethel and Irving Tromberg, George van Cleve, Doug Watts, Lisa Weldon, Francisco Wong-Diaz, Julie Meier Wright, and Joan Zimmerman.

My longtime friend and colleague Brian Runkel went the extra mile, sharing detailed thoughts on various points throughout the book. His contribution is invaluable.

These individuals represent a range of perspectives. Their mention here should not be interpreted as indicating their opinions of the arguments and proposals presented in the book.

My debts to Rachel and Charles Bernheim go far beyond the scope of this project. The dedication is offered as a token of appreciation for their friendship, kindness, and inspiration.

Image Credits

Frontispiece

Archibald Willard, *Yankee Doodle* [later known as *The Spirit of '76*] (ca. 1875). Licensed under public domain via Wikimedia Commons.

Prelude

Thomas Cole, *The Consummation of Empire* (1836). Abbot Hall, Marblehead, Massachusetts. Licensed under public domain via Wikimedia Commons.

Chapter One

James Montgomery Flagg, *Wake Up America! Civilization Calls Every Man, Woman and Child* (New York: The Hegeman Print, 1916). Library of Congress Prints and Photographs Division. Licensed under public domain.

Congressional Budget Office, "Federal Debt Held by the Public" (July 2014). Licensed under public domain.

George Washington University, Regulatory Studies Center, "Total Pages, Code of Federal Regulations (1950–2014)." Used by permission.

Chapter Two

Joseph Keppler, *The Bosses of the Senate, Puck* (23 January 1889). Library of Congress Prints and Photographs Division. Licensed under public domain.

Chapter Three

Udo Keppler, *The Spirit of '08, Puck* (15 May 1907). Library of Congress Prints and Photographs Division. Licensed under public domain.

Chapter Four

The Fruits of Arbitrary Power, or the Bloody Massacre, engraved, printed and sold by Paul Revere, on or about 28 March 1770. The print was copied by Revere from a design by Henry Pelham. Licensed under public domain via Wikimedia Commons.

Coda

Paul Weinberg. *Nelson Mandela Voting, 1994.* [CC BY-SA 3.0 (http://creativecommons.org/licenses/by-sa/3.0) or GFDL (http://www.gnu.org/copyleft/fdl.html)], via Wikimedia Commons.

Sue Ream, *The Fall of the Berlin Wall.* [CC BY 3.0 (http://creativecommons.org/licenses/by/3.0)], via Wikimedia Commons.

Warren K. Leffler, *March on Washington, 28 August 1963.* Licensed under public domain via Wikimedia Commons.

Theodore Roosevelt. Photographer unknown. Library of Congress Prints and Photographs Division. Licensed under public domain via Wikimedia Commons.

About the Author

James Strock is an independent entrepreneur and reformer in business, government, and politics.

Strock founded the Serve to Lead Group in 1997. The company assembles talent to provide a range of services, including in 21st century leadership development; the environmental-social-governance space; and various roles and tasks for corporate, start-up, financial, and not-for-profit enterprises.

He served as the founding secretary of the California Environmental Protection Agency, chief of law enforcement for the US Environmental Protection Agency, general counsel of the US Office of Personnel Management, and special counsel to the US Senate Environment and Public Works Committee.

Strock serves on numerous public and private boards and commissions. He is a member of the Council on Foreign Relations and the Authors Guild, and a trustee of the Theodore Roosevelt Association.

To arrange for James Strock to speak to your organization or event, please visit www.servetolead.org.

49192734R00158

Made in the USA
San Bernardino, CA
16 May 2017